# Get the Ideal Companion
# to Anna's Award-Winning Book at:
# Amazon.com

This Guided Reflection Journal will help you ground the
ideas and concepts in the book, so you can start practicing
how to live a more fulfilling and joyful spiritual life
in our very material world.

# What They're Saying About Anna's First Book

2017 — *Living Now Awards* Bronze Medal Winner (Enlightenment/Spirituality)

"This wise and profound book will help you unite your ordinary life with the laws and visions of your deep spirit."

—Andrew Harvey, Author of *The Hope: A Guide to Sacred Activism*

"*Living a Spiritual Life in a Material World: Four Keys to Fulfillment and Joy* are universal principles that are a guaranteed formula to align your daily actions with the intentions of the Universe. By integrating the spiritual with the material you will gain clarity on your goals and manifest the life you want to live. Use the Four Keys to unlock your innate spiritual power and increase your impact in the world."

—Jack Canfield, Co-Author of *The Success Principles*™ & *Chicken Soup for the Soul*®

"…Impressively well written…an extraordinary self-help instructional guide that will prove to be a life-affirming, life-enhancing, life-enriching read from beginning to end…"

—Midwest Book Review

"It is probably the hardest thing that any of us can do – trying to live a spiritual life in a material world. I admire Gatmon for overcoming a dysfunctional childhood, traveling internationally as a model, marrying and raising two children, becoming a transformative counselor, and being willing to share her insights through this book. The voice that comes through is one that strongly reminds me of people like Eckhart Tolle, Deepak Chopra, Paulo Coelho and Don Miguel Ruiz. These individuals present us with ways of living our lives that bring our spiritual life into alignment with our daily life."

—Bonnie Cehovet, Certified Tarot Grand
Master, Reiki Master/Teacher, and writer

"Inspiring and practical *Living a Spiritual Life in a Material World* provides a clear and innovative program for spiritual growth and enlightenment."

—William Bloom, PhD, Founder of Spiritual
Companions Trust, Author of *The Endorphin
Effect and The Power of the New Spirituality*

"…Anna Gatmon presents Spirituality 101 for all readers wishing to accelerate their spiritual development. Well done."

—Library Journal

"This is not the typical how-to-achieve-spirituality book, but another creature altogether. Have a read and you may well find yourself in another sphere of perception, one that will send you along a path toward something of great value for you."

—John Grinder, Co-Creator of
Neuro-Linguistic Programing (NLP)

"What an uplifting read! Anna's insights into spiritual living are illuminated by her sincere and generous accounts from her own life. In my position, I am constantly working to bridge spiritual values and practices with material practicalities. The "4 Keys" presented in this book have been a meaningful support in integrating these two."

—Jonathan Fisher, CEO, Homes Place Group

# SHIFT CALLING

## A PRACTICAL GUIDE TO ACCELERATE YOUR SPIRITUAL GROWTH

# SHIFT CALLING

## A PRACTICAL GUIDE TO ACCELERATE
## YOUR SPIRITUAL GROWTH

## ANNA GATMON, PHD

Published by Expansive Press.
*Shift Calling: A Practical Guide to Accelerate Your Spiritual Growth*
Print ISBN: 979-8-218-25550-3
E-ISBN: 979-8-218-25551-0



Front cover photo by Melba Estilla.

*May these times call you to greatness,
and may this book show you the way.*

# Contents

# Introduction

*"When nothing is sure,*
*everything is possible."*

—Margaret Drabble

When COVID-19 hit the world in 2020, it was a shift calling on a global magnitude that none of us had experienced before. We each had to deal with the effects of this monumental shift in whatever way it showed up in our life, with our individual circumstances. We were each faced with our mortality and the possibility, or tragic actuality, of losing loved ones. The fear of death and a total disruption of our habitual lifestyle brought tremendous anxiety regarding what the future holds. But it also offered us a gift in disguise, a shift calling us to examine our values, so we could make more conscious choices about what matters in life and how we want to live and care for each other.

While nature seemed to thrive with the sudden drop in pollution and wildlife began to expand its habitat, we humans faced important dilemmas individually and collectively. Some issues propelled us into greater disagreement, while others opened up new possibilities for making changes in our private lives and our society.

A year after lockdown, the great resignation occurred in the United States, where tens of millions of Americans quit their jobs in search of working conditions that would bring them greater professional respect and a renewed sense of purpose. It seemed that if life, as we knew it, could radically shift overnight, then maybe other shifts were possible as well. Maybe we could take charge of our life and make different choices that would be more affirming and fulfilling. So, while tens of millions resigned from their jobs, each had to summon their courage, take a leap of faith, and make a brave new choice without knowing what the future would bring. But it seemed enough to know that the present wasn't good enough anymore. And so, a wave of individual courage turned into a national shift toward living more meaningful lives.

The vaccination debate ignited complex moral issues such as personal freedom and self-determination versus the collective welfare of our communities. We had to grapple with where we stand on this issue. We had to face our self-righteousness, as we often felt we held the ultimate truth. While this debate produced extreme divisiveness in local and national communities, it also highlighted that, for the first time in history, humanity was sharing a common global event, even if we each were affected by it in unique ways. So, it was also a reminder that we are connected and interdependent, that we share the same planet, that we need each other, and that we have to work together to solve local and global issues. It was a quantum shift in our perspective, moving from a mindset of pure self-interest to one of collective consideration.

Extreme climate crises around the world, such as fires, floods, storms, and droughts, keep driving this message home even more and awaken us to our shared humanity and destiny.

I perceive all that is going on, the challenges and the shifts forward, as part of a spiritual awakening of the highest order. Granted, we still have a long way to go, but the world pandemic and everything that ensued from it offer us the opportunity to radically shift our perception of ourselves. Can we learn to recognize that we are part of a global village, living together on a finite planet?

Technological advances make us a global village. What happens in one part of the world affects us, one way or another, whether it is a war, which affects the world economy, or the murder of an innocent black man captured on video, which goes viral and cracks our hearts open, instigating a global movement of outrage against racism and police brutality. These shifts call us to awaken to our shared humanity, common destiny, life's precious-ness, and the need to take care of the planet that sustains us.

Einstein said that we cannot solve a problem from the same mindset or consciousness from which it was created. That means that we need to shift something in our way of thinking and relating to the world to come up with solutions to our existing problems. Jack Welch, the former chairman and CEO of General Electric, said, "If the rate of change on the outside exceeds the rate of change on the inside, the end is near." While he was referring to organizations needing to change internally to adapt to external conditions, this principle is true for us at this time in history. We need to shift internally to effectuate external change. And we need to accelerate the rate of our internal shifting to catch up with the rate at which our material and technological world is evolving. In other words, we need to *grow at the speed of life*, as life is changing rapidly.

I believe that we need a spiritual shift where we expand our perception of ourselves from just humans to wondrous and creative spiritual beings. We also need to alter our perspective of nature and our world from separation and isolation to connection and wholeness. And to do that, we need potent spiritual principles that will allow us to solve our problems from a more expansive mindset and wiser conscious awareness than the one that has brought us to this point in our life.

The good news is that even a small, one-degree shift will alter your trajectory. That is why this book offers many different shifts that you can consider and practice. Some focus on shifting your perception of yourself, some on shifting your perspective of the world, and others on shifting your probabilities for accelerating your spiritual growth. All of them will provide you with the most effective and powerful tools and practices to make the internal shifts you need to experience the external changes that will bring you greater joy, meaning, and purpose and elevate humanity and our planet.

*Are you ready to join me on this journey to accelerate your spiritual growth and transform your life and our world?*

# Part I: What Shifts Called Me

*"Don't ask what the world needs.*
*Ask what makes you come alive and go do it.*
*Because what the world needs*
*are people who have come alive."*

—Howard Thurman

# A Shift in My Perception:
# From Unworthy to Deserving

Life seemed unfair growing up. I had thick, bushy red hair and freckles dotting every inch of my pale white skin that covered an unusually tall and lanky body. There was both alcohol and rage in my family, and by age 15, my parents had separated. My home as a teenager felt more like a jail cell where I served time under the tutelage of a cruel stepmother and domineering father. My alcoholic mother lost custody over my two younger siblings, and I was old enough to be asked who I wanted to live with. As I was angry at my mother for her drinking, I chose to live with my father, thinking it was the lesser of two evils. I had a severe stutter and undiagnosed learning challenges, which, combined with the emotional challenges I was facing at home, resulted in poor performance at school. So, I spent summers during high school studying for exams that would allow me to graduate to the next level. I was grounded, locked up inside, and unable to leave my dysfunctional home setting. I was more than an ugly duckling. I was a captive alien without a clue about life or how to succeed—a victim of circumstances.

Living in Israel meant my future would include joining the army at 18 years old for two years, which was mandatory. Beyond that, I had no hope for anything better. Nine months before enlisting, after I finally graduated from high school, my father allowed me to visit my mother, who was living in Sweden. That's when I heard my first shift calling.

While accompanying a friend to the pharmacy one Saturday morning, I took my seat in the waiting area. I wore a bulky blue sweater, no makeup, and a red mop for a hairdo. A few minutes passed, and I raised my gaze to notice a woman watching my every move.

While I fidgeted in my chair, she got up and approached me. "Excuse me; I'm sorry for staring at you. But I just have to ask, would you like to travel the world and work as a fashion model?"

Flabbergasted, I asked, "Me?" I had to double-check. After all, maybe the woman was waiting for a vision check.

"Yes, YOU!" she said.

It appeared she saw something I could not see for myself, even when I looked at myself in the mirror.

Within two months, I met a renowned fashion modeling agent who wanted to send me to Paris to try my luck. I simply could not believe what I was hearing. I was supposed to wear army fatigues, not modeling clothes, in front of a camera in Paris, the world capital of fashion. Then, he said something that would stick with me for the rest of my life.

"Anna, if you want to get something, you have to give something."

Despite my insecurities, I decided to give up on my duty to serve in the Israeli army and give up my low self-esteem to pursue a career in modeling. It may sound like a simple choice, but for someone who believed she was ugly, awkward, and dumb, I had to muster all the courage I had to make this leap of faith with no guarantees. In addition, I had grown up in Israel and truly believed that enlisting in military service at age 18 was my duty to my country. My dad had been a pilot in the air force, and I felt like a traitor if I didn't join the army. I thought my friends in Israel would judge me for skipping my military service. It was not a simple decision for me to make, as much as it may seem a no-brainer for you reading this today. But I saw this opportunity to free myself and, maybe, change my destiny. So, I leaped into the unknown and was whisked away to Paris for a chance to be on the cover of *16 Magazine,* just a few months after being discovered at the pharmacy.

The fashion world was looking for something other than the typical blonde with blue eyes. One photo shoot led to another, and soon I was gracing the pages of *Elle* and *Marie Claire*, among other fashion magazines. I would come to represent several popular brands over the next ten-year career. There was no going back.

This was no small shift in my identity. I went from a cooped-up, self-hating, red-headed teenager with low self-esteem and a severe stutter to walking the runways of Yves Saint Laurent and Jean Paul Gautier. It was an unimaginable change from hiding in my room while my father and stepmother screamed at one of us kids.

While no amount of external shift can provide deep healing for the traumas I went through as a child, the process of leaving behind my home, country, friends, and my life as I knew it provided a radical change of circumstances. It was enough for me to begin perceiving myself in a bigger and more life-affirming way than I was led to believe by my parents and teachers at school. I began to be treated with respect and paid handsomely for my work, which shifted my self-perception. Through this journey, I shed everything I had believed about myself while taking on a new perception that aligned more with who I truly was. I was not only a glamorous high fashion model. I became free to enjoy the process of discovering myself and my limitless potential.

*Can you remember a time in your life when you shifted your self-perception? How did it change your life?*

# A Shift in My Perspective:
# From Victim to Empowered

After only two weeks of attending first grade at a local public school, my oldest son had already lost the joy of going to school. A few mornings a week, he'd ask to stay home, and I'd have a difficult time convincing him that he had no choice but to get up and go. Only a few months earlier, when he was still in kindergarten, he used to skip and hum every morning when I'd drop him off and every afternoon when I'd pick him up. Now, that spark in his eyes was fading. When I'd drop him off and pick him up, he looked despondent, a far cry from the beautiful, big soul for a son that I knew. He slouched, carrying his overloaded backpack. Something was off, but I couldn't put my finger on what.

Whatever "it" was, it got worse every day. It was like watching a butterfly recoil into a cocoon. His growth was transforming backward. At this young age, I feared his future would be negatively impacted by bottoming-out self-esteem. I started to question the school itself. My spouse and I had wanted to send our son to an acclaimed school nearby, but that turned out to be impossible due to municipality politics. Without a better option, we sent him to our local public school.

I began to see myself, and my past self, in my son. And that wasn't acceptable. I needed a shift in perspective. I had just completed my doctorate studies which focused on creating the best conditions for transformative learning in individuals and groups, helping me heal from my own disastrous first 12 years of school. In short, I knew better. I knew how to provide my son with an education that would stay with him for life, but we were confined to the public school system.

Homeschooling was a new concept in the year 2000 in Israel, but I was intrigued. So, I found a family who was leading a homeschooling program. I reached out and spoke to the mother who was happy to help me out. After a few minutes of sharing my concerns about my son's school, I asked, point blank, "How do you homeschool?"

"We don't homeschool. We unschool," she said.

Through the conversation, I learned that "unschooling" was a concept developed by the American educator John Holt, a proponent of homeschooling and pioneer of the unschooling method. Holt defined unschooling as a style of home education that allows your child's interests and curiosities, combined with a rich variety of resources, to drive the learning path. Rather than using a defined curriculum, unschoolers trust children to gain knowledge organically. I thought this had potential and that I could take it one step further. Because I believe that life provides all the learning opportunities we could ask for, we could make life our classroom. The world would become an encyclopedia, and every moment, a platform for learning.

That seemed like a radical shift in perspective from the traditional frontal instruction and rote learning model of the public school system, and yet, on some deep level, it seemed to make total sense to me. I felt confident I could provide many wonderful ways to learn by doing life together. And so we began.

Cooking in the kitchen taught my son about math, fractions, chemistry, and how to follow recipes to create delicious foods. A visit to the park gave us a gymnasium for exercise, a chance to learn about nature, and an opportunity to develop social skills. When we traveled, we learned history, geography, and language. While shopping, we learned about money, math, and the economy. When my son showed interest in a particular topic, we pursued it. While we drove around doing errands, he read out loud the street signs. By the time he was seven years old, he was fluent in both Hebrew and English.

It didn't take long for me to create a model, a visual roadmap for home—or unschooling—that parents could follow. It gave me a blueprint for my work and allowed me to see progress and catch challenges.

With my educational framework as my guide, even playing with Legos offered me insight into many skills and learning opportunities. For example, a child has to imagine a desired outcome, make a plan, and exhibit determination to build the vision block by block. They learn spatial orientation, abstract thinking, focus, and delaying gratification. Legos can be a metaphor for life. Children must persevere through challenges and be resourceful, flexible, and creative. They must build self-esteem and confidence, taking ownership of the project and related pitfalls. The child seems to be "just playing," but they're learning real-world skills and valuable intangibles that apply to life.

I share all this with you to give you an idea of the significant shift in perspective I went through when I moved from the traditional public school system to unschooling my children.

My son thrived from this new way of learning, and I felt the rewards of watching the process. My big-souled butterfly of a son could spread his wings and fly. And I got to create the conditions for this to happen. I also witnessed developmental milestones, like when my younger son had a pivotal breakthrough in his independence and level of confidence.

My younger son, an infant when we began homeschooling, was born into our family's lifestyle of breastfeeding, sharing a family bed, and being together all day, engaged in different family activities. I'd hang out with my younger son in the shallow waters when we'd go to his older brother's weekly swimming classes. The waters were deep enough that I could bend my knees and immerse myself up to my neck. My son would cling to me like a monkey, not confident enough to let go and venture out on his own, although he had armbands to keep him afloat. But one time, his toes coincidentally touched the bottom of the pool. I could see his face light up at the revelation that he could stand on his own two feet and be independent. As soon as he realized this, he gently pushed me away and began exploring the shallow pool. From then on, he was off swimming in the pool and discovering his new relationship with his body in water. It was amazing to witness this realization of independence and the beginning of self-mastery. It was a short instant in the pool but a significant learning milestone.

Over the years, my family's educational path had many more twists and turns, but the most important thing was that we adapted to our family's and my children's needs. While homeschooling was the right choice for my family for a few years, it is not the right path for everyone. Like everything, it has its challenges and rewards. The point is that this shift in perspective around how significant learning can happen in a natural home environment opened our eyes to possibilities previously confined by mainstream educational thinking. For us, it opened up a whole new way of being a family, and I can proudly say today that my two children have become fine and compassionate young adults who are free thinkers and care deeply about the plight of others and the state of our world.

The initial reason for homeschooling was to give my children the best education I could provide at the time. But in the process, I discovered how much I loved being a full-time mom. I was present at critical milestones of my children's development, which gave me such pleasure. And I also discovered that I am an educator at heart. I got to express my calling by developing my original educational model that we followed as a family, which later became the basis for an alternative elementary school I founded. And so this major shift in perspective became a significant breakthrough in my personal and professional development.

That is the power I have found in taking big leaps of faith when external circumstances force us to shift. Once we take that leap of faith and change the course of our actions, every-thing seems to come together for the greater good. We and our world are transformed in the process.

*What fundamental beliefs have you been forced to question, and how did doing so affect your life?*

# A Shift in My Probabilities:
# From Drifting Along to
# Finding My Calling

Although shifts may be calling, you will miss them if you're not listening. Listening requires a willingness to engage with these impulses that try to draw our attention from our habitual day-to-day life. And timing is also crucial. Sometimes we are not quite ready to hear the shift calling. But listening to and acting on such impulses can lead to major changes—for good.

I wasn't particularly interested the first time I heard about the spiritual community, eco-village, and education center of Findhorn in Northern Scotland, known today as the Findhorn Foundation and community. It had become famous in the early sixties for its gardens, where the founders used spiritual princi-ples to grow forty-pound cabbages in barren sandy soil in the Findhorn Bay Caravan Park. I was in my mid-thirties at the time and showed no interest in the famous Findhorn gardens or their spiritual philosophy.

A decade later, in my mid-forties, a friend told me again about Findhorn and praised the community, saying that I had to visit. She was enamored with the place, so I was polite and kind but didn't think much of it. A few months later, she called me and said excitedly, "One of the original co-founders of the Findhorn Community is coming to Israel for the first time and giving a three-day workshop. You have to come." She insisted I join her. This time, something inside me felt that way too. I was homeschooling at the time, so I had to find a babysitter.

"I'll commit to going for one day," I said. If nothing else, I would satisfy my curiosity. After attending one day of the workshop, I asked the babysitter for two more days because I became fascinated with the Findhorn story and philosophy.

By my mid-forties, I had been exposed to the 12 Steps Recovery Program for over a decade. My mother had gone into recovery for her alcoholism, and I had joined different 12-step programs for children and families. I was okay talking about a "Higher Power" but didn't connect it to anything religious, and spirituality was a word that didn't exist in my vocabulary.

But all that changed after I attended this three-day workshop. Suddenly, I was hooked. I seemed to resonate deeply with the two central teachings of the Findhorn Foundation. The first one is that each one of us can have a direct, unmediated connection with the Divine, Source, God, or however you relate to the force that creates worlds. This relationship can happen by connecting with our inner divinity. As we are a direct expression of this same Divine force, communicating with it is accessible to all of us without a religious mediator. The second teaching is that nature has consciousness with which we can engage, communicate, and collaborate, as they were doing in the Findhorn gardens. I elaborate on these teachings in Part IV: Shifting Your Probabilities to Accelerate Your Spiritual Growth. These two teachings rocked my world and have since taken me on a significant spiritual journey. While I didn't know at the time the profound influence these two teachings would have on my personal and professional life, something in me resonated deeply with them. This time, I was ready and listened to the shift calling me. I'd even go as far as to say that I was on fire and felt the urge to enlist others.

I dragged my family and close friends to Scotland for a week-long Findhorn Foundation Family Experience workshop. And only two months after that, I found myself, again, on a plane to Scotland for a two-week workshop called Falling in Love with God with that same original co-founder, Dorothy Maclean and her colleague Judy McAllister. One of the guided meditations in that two-week workshop, an exercise appropriately called The Doorway, prompted a huge shift in perspective regarding my beliefs about spirituality, God, and religion. I relay the full experience and exercise in my first book, *Living a Spiritual Life in a Material World*, as this simple guided meditation turned out to be a major shift in perspective. Over the next two decades, it evolved into a quantum shift in personal and professional probabilities.

After this workshop, universal spiritual principles became the focus of my doctoral dissertation, where I developed four universal principles I named The Four Keys to Spiritual-Material Wholeness. Just one profoundly simple discovery

I made, what I have come to call, The Expansive Principle, which I talk about in Part IV of this book, multiplied my probabilities for personal happiness and professional fulfillment.

Following my dissertation was my first book and numerous speaking events where I shared the findings from my doctoral study. Building on that, the teachings I share with you in this book synthesize the insights and deep understanding I have gained in the last few years as I continued studying the nature of reality, the evolution of human consciousness, and how to live in greater peace, joy, and harmony on our planet.

Almost two decades have passed since that guided meditation in a workshop at the Findhorn Foundation. During this time, I have listened to many shifts that have guided me along the way. I have discovered my own spiritual path and developed my own spiritual teachings, which I further develop in this book. And I have come to realize and acknowledge that my spiritual journey and teachings are a continuation of the lineage of the teachings and principles I was first introduced to at the Findhorn Foundation.

It all began with a shift in perspective, which would lead to a considerable shift in my probabilities to accelerate my spiritual growth as I developed my teachings about a much bigger, more wondrous, and mystical side of life. I found a hidden spiritual world, another realm with different laws, which I could access. It was like discovering a superpower. No longer was God a mystery that only certain people could speak to and hear from. God is accessible. The planet is not inanimate. It's alive, operating with a self-regulating system and a consciousness with which we can collaborate.

My probability of living a fulfilling, successful life had been drastically improved through this single shift. From this premise, a pathway was laid for the rest of my life. I found purpose and a life with meaning. I was once stuck at home with low self-esteem, but I answered the shift that would change my perception of myself. Then, I shifted my worldview and changed how my family and I would experience education. And finally, my eyes were opened to a spiritual shift that forever changed my life calling and probabilities for meaningful transformation.

*Can you think of a significant shift you've gone through which has had a compounding effect on your life?*

# A Shift in My Path Onward: My COVID Resolution

Death hovered as the world feared what would become of us due to the COVID-19 outbreak in the Spring of 2020. Questions about the contagion were on everyone's mind as quarantines were announced worldwide. *How do you catch COVID? What are the symptoms? What are the chances of survival should we get COVID? Do we really have to stay cooped up at home, and for how long?*

Like most, I had to sit with death knocking on my door. *How long would I have if I caught the virus? How would I say goodbye to my dearest loved ones? How would I face death when it came to take me?*

I found myself thinking of all of this one morning while standing in my living room, looking out at a beautiful valley lined with apple orchards and vineyards. The view was expansive, and so I began to feel a sense of spaciousness in my being. It was a familiar feeling of great joy, and my body felt like it was floating in a timeless space. I had come to recognize this as an expansion of my consciousness.

I first noticed this feeling when I chose to move to Paris, France, to work as a fashion model and, then again, during that workshop at the Findhorn Foundation when I had my so-called spiritual awakening. At the time, I would have described myself as high on life, full of excitement, and very present. As I began studying this state of being during my doctoral research, I discovered I could induce this spacious feeling intentionally, which was the most empowering and liberating feeling of delight. I seemed to be able to shift from feeling down to uplifted within minutes. I also realized that when I got into one of these expansive states, I'd be flooded with a stream of meaningful insights about whatever I was dealing with. Eventually, I identified four universal principles that became the focus of my dissertation and my first book, *Expansive Presence, Attentive Listening, Inspired Action*, and *Faith-Filled Knowing*.

Here I was that morning, looking out at the valley outside my backyard, thinking of death. Despite the foreboding circumstances, my mood had shifted unexpectedly, and within minutes, a deep sense of gratitude washed over me. I realized I was in one of those expansive moments when I was about to tap into a wise, spiritual perspective on life and death. As I listened attentively, a stream of thoughts flooded me at great speed.

*I have lived an amazing life. In fact, I have lived a uniquely extraordinary life. I'm so appreciative of the amazing experiences I've had on so many levels. I've made hard decisions, but each one saved my life. I love who I've become. I have been deeply loved and have learned to love unconditionally. And I have had profound spiritual realizations that have helped* transform my life and the life of the people I have touched. So, if I were to pass on to the other side now, I would be fine with that. While there is always more I could do and would want to explore, I have lived a full life into my early sixties and am content with what I have lived through. So, I am okay to go if my time has come to leave this plane.

As if some hidden force led me, I was then reminded of some harsher moments in my life. I didn't want to go there as it was still painful after so many decades, but admittedly, I had felt like I was drowning in despair so many times. My past wounding swelled up to overtake my hard-earned sense of identity and purpose. It was like I reverted to that insecure, ugly duckling with an alcoholic parent, destined to join the Israeli military. Suddenly, I felt hopeless, as if my life was doomed from the beginning. From this perspective, the cards life dealt me added up to suffering.

I imagined how my mother must have felt because I betrayed her when I chose to live with my father, even though I believed that decision was the best of two evils. My father and stepmother were cruel, doling out the harshness of the Israeli culture. I thought of my anorexic tendencies of starving my emotions because it was unsafe to feel, and no adult in my life could mediate all the traumas I was experiencing. I remembered the first time I finished a full meal, as I had promised my sponsor. I was overcome with sadness, feeling how lonely I had felt as a child. There were all the times my mother was drunk, unconscious on the floor, and I had to take care of my siblings while my father was off working. And that horrible time when my father was raging out of control, kicking my brother, lying on the floor, in the belly, while the rest of us kids hid terrified in our rooms. And then all the days I had woken up as an adult, even after I had my own family, feeling hopeless and worthless. And how I'd have to work myself out of this mood to meet the day's demands.

Here I was, during the early days of lockdown, thinking of all I had endured and all the pain I had caused. I thought of the senseless suffering in the world. At that moment, life seemed to have no meaning. After all, being liberated from the suffering in this world seemed like the best choice.

Then again, my thoughts drifted to what would happen after death. Now, I believe that when we leave our bodies and this world, the essence of who we are just walks over to another dimension of existence, a non-physical reality. It may sound simple, but that is what I have been shown happens at the moment of transition. In that non-physical state of conscious-ness, we have easier access to reality's expansive, blissful nature, what we often call the spiritual world. That's the expan-sive state I spoke of discovering during my doctoral research, which we also have access to in this world.

And that brought me back to thinking what a wonderful adventure life is on planet Earth. Something inside me started renewing my mind. I remembered being a joyous little girl running free in my grandfather's garden, playing until dark, picking apples from the trees, and pulling carrots from the ground. I'd dust them off, wash them in the little pond, and eat them without a care. That was my Garden of Eden.

I remembered loving to sing as a child. I'd take an empty toilet tissue roll, make a hole for a string, pretend it was a microphone, and perform for the family in the living room. I still had this beautiful, joyous little girl I wanted to bring back into existence in my life. Like everyone else, I want to enjoy life, live with a sense of purpose, be happy, have meaningful relationships, and feel like I belong. Through this moment, I was engaging in a shift in my path onward.

I believe we have come forth into this life to connect the spiritual and material realms and bring them into one sacred wholeness. The challenge we face is how to create a solid, stable bridge between these two realms of life so that we can travel with greater ease from our pain and suffering to our joy and liberation. That is what I hope this book will provide for you—a bridge between the realms. And I believe whatever shift calls you is your cue to embark on this sacred adventure.

My COVID resolution? My inner guides have told me, "We have shown you the kingdom. Now claim it and share it with others." So, as we co-journey through life, you on your path and me on mine, my resolve is to provide the map and tools for us to build this bridge in our lifetime.

***Does my story bring forth any particular resolve in you?***

# How to Work With This Book

I've organized this book into different parts, each offering unique ways to make shifts in your life. This includes various categories of shifts, all of which will accelerate your spiritual growth. I conclude with shifting your path onward, which applies the different shifts in the book to common areas in our life. Each part is divided into chapters, discussing some of the most significant shifts within each category. At the end of each chapter, I offer a question to connect you back to the shifts calling you. Finally, at the end of each part of the book, I offer a reflection prompt to help you integrate the suggestions into your life.

Take the time to consider each new idea, seeing how you can adapt it to fit your unique life circumstances. Knowledge isn't powerful unless it's acted upon and experienced firsthand. Through direct personal experience, you will come into the presence of the truth, wisdom, and power of the ideas and suggestions in this book. Through direct experience, you can adapt these to fit your unique needs and circumstances. The good news is that if you take action, I'm confident the ideas and suggestions I share with you in the coming pages can deliver significant and sustainable shifts with benefits that will compound over time.

You will benefit the most from this book by meditating on each suggestion, practicing it, and integrating it before moving on to the following chapter. Ultimately, the goal is to incorporate new ideas and practices into your life. In doing so, you can experience the inner shifts you need to make to realize the external changes you desire.

Listen to what shift is calling you and start there. Whatever shift you decide to take on, you will experience that making small incremental changes will, over time, add up to a significant improvement. Shifts have profound and compounding outcomes which can bring greater meaning and purpose to your life as they liberate you from those sleepless nights and that which keeps you hostage.

Below is the step-by-step process for shifting your life onward, which I will walk you through in the forthcoming parts of this book:

- *What Shift is Calling You* — As the title suggests, we begin by helping you identify where you are, where you want to be, and what may be holding you back. This part sets the stage for the spiritual work of shift-making, understanding the underlying dynamics of shifting, and how you can begin perceiving your challenges as opportunities for spiritual growth.
- *The Practice of Shift-Making* — Here, we lay out some definitions related to shift-making and how

you can use them as you heed the shift calling you. Shifting is not a one-time event but a craft you get better at the more you practice. So, you'll gain a helpful understanding of how a one-degree shift has the power to redirect your destination and how the practice of shift-making can integrate your personal, inner work, your spiritual work, and your impact on the world.

- *Shifting Your Probabilities to Accelerate Your Spiritual Growth* — We want to increase the probability and scale of your shift by working with universal principles that will guide you at critical points during the process. These will compound your transformation—small fundamental shifts will become big transformations in your life. Without shifting your probabilities, you may be unable to sustain the shifts you are trying to make. Growth occurs while living your life and shifting to a greater version of yourself.

- *Shifting Your Perception of Yourself* — The most powerful work we can do is our work on ourselves. One major step forward is to shift your perception of yourself, which impacts your identity and expands your sense of self. You can't make any shift by protecting the same mindset that got you where you are today. In this part, I will share how to envision yourself as a growing, enlightened portal that gains and shares wisdom and how your identity contains the power to make positive changes in your life and the world around you.

- *Shifting Your Perspective of the World* — The next step focuses on shifting your perspective to a more honest and loving viewpoint. Too often, the perspective you hold about your life produces the stalemate you're experiencing. There are fundamental fallacies at work that keep you stuck. Yet, there are counter truths that can open new possibilities for you, with far-reaching positive implications. Let's reveal the perspective holding you back and replace it with a new way of looking at people, places, and things, in addition to how you perceive your own situation. These little shifts can extract you from the limitations of your current situation.

- *Shifting Your Path Onwards* — Once you've begun shifting in any of these areas, your path onward will naturally flow in more expansive, compassionate, and intentional ways. You can nurture shifts in your path in specific areas of your life. These include at home, at work, in your relationship to money and wealth, your health and well-being, your primary relationships, your connection to nature, and your impact in the world.

***Is there a part of this book that you are instinctively drawn to more than others?***

# Reflection Prompt

Take a moment to reflect on different events in your life. What moments feel like significant shifts that altered the course of your life? In what way did they provide a significant shift? Was it a shift in your identity and how you perceived yourself, or a significant shift in perspective or the values you hold? In what ways did it influence the people who were part of your life at the time? Take a moment to acknowledge your experiences, courage, spirit of adventure, and faith. While life calls us to wake up and show up, it takes our willingness to play along, shed old ways that don't serve us anymore, and embrace new ways of becoming more of who we truly are. You have come a long way. And you are about to embark on an adventure to shift your life by accelerating your spiritual growth.

# Part II: What Shift Is Calling You?

*"There's about to be a shift in your life.*
*Get ready for your blessings.*
*You've been through enough*
*and a breakthrough is on the way.*
*Don't doubt it. Just claim it!*

—Tony Gaskin

# Answering the Call

Tell me, what keeps you up at night, wondering how you can resolve it? Does it have to do with a conflict in a significant relationship, your finances, a health issue, a work situation, or something related to living a more purpose-filled life? How many times have you run through different scenarios of that situation and how you got to where you are, recounting the dialogue in your mind, only to find yourself repeating, again and again, the same thoughts as you find your mood spiraling? By now, it seems impossible to fall asleep, and you wonder how you'll get through the day ahead with so few hours of rest. I've been there.

Is there an area in your life that seems to always present challenges? You may suffer from chronic health problems, ongoing financial hardships, unfulfilling work circumstances, or the seeming inability to enjoy ongoing intimacy with a romantic partner or your growing children. What doesn't seem to go away, even though you've been working at it? What keeps rearing its ugly head in different situations? You can also ask yourself, *What is the biggest gap between where I am and where I want to be?*

Maybe your distress goes beyond your personal life and affects a social group you belong to, a community, or an identity you share with many others being targeted. Perhaps, an injustice enrages you about a cause you care deeply about. You may be experiencing collective trauma that keeps being reported in the news, affecting your personal life and your people.

Maybe you are just anxious about looming ecological disasters, future pandemics, and whether we will make it as a species or destroy ourselves before we get a chance to wake up to the bountiful planet we live on. This anxiety can lead to fears about the precious and miraculous children born every day who will inherit today's generational curses. Despite the creative solutions generated to save our planet and all of us who call it our home, you may feel helpless.

I'm going to stop before you decide to put this book down, saying to yourself, *I can relate to many of these, but it's overwhelming. I feel like it's coming at me from all directions. Is there any hopeful message?*

I'm glad you asked. Here's the thing. I believe that anything that feels like it's tormenting you is a calling from deep within your innermost soul to make a shift, grow, and undergo a profound transformation into the person you are capable of being.

Could this repeated suffering be a friend calling you to wake up and do what you can to improve your life for yourself, your loved ones, and our world? Because I believe a small shift can lead to massive change.

It's time to answer this call. I believe when we feel stuck in a rut, helpless, incapable, or lacking potential, it's a shift calling from within, saying, *let's shift what keeps calling you again and again. There's still time and opportunity to shift and grow (emotionally, spiritually, mentally, physically, and socially) and become the best and most empowered version of yourself. I am your most precious ally, and I am not going away until you heed my call and use this moment to make a quantum leap in your life.*

In this book, I will outline the principles behind the potential shift you could make. But I want you to find more than advice on how to change your life. At the core, all the shifts I propose are spiritual shifts, as they offer you an expansive perspective on your life and the world. Once you engage with them, they have the power to accelerate your spiritual growth and inspire powerful change toward a joy-filled life of meaning and purpose for yourself and your world.

***What area in your life do you most long to address and shift at this time?***

# Desire is Required

Desire is the first and most crucial step in any shift you wish to make. Without desiring something, you'll have no inspiration or motivation to take action and make any change. So that's where we must begin when we want to change our life and, as a result, our world. Desire can come in different forms, so don't judge yourself for how it shows up. You may experience a deep longing for something you've never had and want, more than anything, to believe is possible. You might yearn to stop doing something that is harming you without really knowing how or what to replace it with. You might crave something just because you wish to have a particular experience and see whether you can achieve it. And you might aspire to expand on who you already are or have more of something you already have, amplifying and growing its presence in your life.

What is it you desire? Do you wish for something related to your health, overall well-being, financial circumstances, work, or family? Or does it have to do with your self-esteem and desire for more confidence and courage?

Welcome your desires in whatever form they show up for you. It may not be easy to allow yourself to honor your desires because of how "desire" has been labeled as a negative trait in some cultures and traditions. We are told that mastery over our desires will liberate us from the shackles of being human. So, it may be confusing to feel all these desires swell up within you while your mind might be fighting each such desire, trying to push it back into your unconscious. I say, dismiss those fears, embrace and engage your desires.

Let's bring in an authority on this matter and settle this issue here and now so that you can develop a new relationship with your desires as they direct you toward meaningful and gratifying shifts in your life. The Dalai Lama says, and I'm paraphrasing, that desire in itself is not bad. For example, you may desire to grow your compassion toward others or experience greater inner peace or happiness for yourself and others. You may desire to feel more creative or empowered to share your unique vision in your work setting, find greater ease and playfulness in your relationships, or more harmony in your parenting. Without these desires, we would not grow spiritually, emotionally, professionally, or socially. So many wonderful unique desires deserve to be fulfilled in your personal and professional life, whether big or small, and whether they include a vision for others or just relate to your life. The sky is the limit. So, let's celebrate our desires.

I'm not suggesting we get addicted to our desires or become overly consumed with pursuing them. But desire does play a powerful role in our inspiration to make a shift and ultimately change our world. Our desires run our life when we continually deny or resist them. And they also run our life when we keep wanting more and more but never stop to appreciate what we have and what we have accomplished. In either case, denying or overindulging in our desires runs our lives, and we end up feeling like we can never find peace of mind and contentment. Whether we deny or overindulge in our desires, we deprive ourselves of deep joy and true happiness, which we all deserve to experience.

I know that it's not always easy to discern whether your desires are negatively running your life or whether you are in charge of what you want. After all, who is going to be the judge of that? If you have tried to change your life situation for a long time without much success, does that mean that your desire to change is running your life or that you just haven't given up on wanting a better life for yourself?

Without knowing your particular circumstances, I would say that you just haven't fulfilled the need underlying your desire. You might be trying to change the external symptom to no avail because you are not listening attentively to an underlying need that will not disappear until you address it. So, while we all have some compulsory desires that run our life, I would err on the side of trusting your desires and befriending them more. Discover what underlying need they represent and then work toward answering this essential need rather than trying to control your external behavior. If you shift internally first, external change will happen with greater ease and flow.

Work at the speed of trust. Don't try to force anything. But promise me that if you have an impulse to laugh at the many desires that begin knocking at your door, asking you to consider them as your next shift calling, you will stand up and dance happily. If that happens, welcome them and get acquainted with what they want from you. Savor this moment.

*What desire is asking for your full attention at this moment, and what underlying need wants to be fulfilled?*

# Allowing is Essential

The other day I was reflecting on the different things I've been able to manifest throughout my life and those that I have not been able to manifest. I thought of how good it felt when I realized a dream or a goal and how utterly devastating it had been when I could not make it happen. I wondered, *what was the difference between what I did when I could manifest and what happened when I could not.*

I want to share with you what happens when I am unable to manifest because you might be experiencing something similar. As I want you to take action and make a shift in your life for the better, this might be helpful. It is essential to know what is stopping you from heeding the shift calling you; otherwise, you will just stay stuck and get even more disappointed in yourself and the world. You will just feel more forsaken and doubt yourself even more.

So, here's what happens when I am stuck and cannot move beyond where I'm at: I am just too scared to take the first step toward making it happen! Why is that? Because to take action toward what I so desire, I have to take a risk. I have to feel hopeful that it might happen. Somewhere inside me, I have to believe it is possible; otherwise, why would I take any action? But here's the interesting thing: I tell myself that it will be soul-crushing if I take action and don't experience the dream I long for or the transformation I desire. And I wouldn't be able to bear the disappointment. So, in those situations when I don't take action, I prefer to stay stuck where I am, disappointed that I will never get what I want but relieved I haven't gotten my hopes up and then crushed again. At least it's familiar. Painful, but familiar.

Does it make any sense? I know, it sounds crazy: I already feel what I fear I'll feel if I try and fail. Do you ever feel this way?

It's a big "ah-ha" moment when you realize you are already experiencing what you most fear might happen if you take action. Because what you want is so dear and important to you that you are protecting yourself. You might tell yourself, *At least if I remain in my current situation, I can ignore the pain and heartache because I have learned to live with it and accept it as my reality.* While this is understandable, it is also how we become the prison guards of our own prison.

When you realize this, you can stay emotionally stuck in a familiar situation or open up to the opportunity that change is possible and that the shift calling you is inviting you to transform your life.

Have you ever thought about what happens when you have dared to make a shift and succeeded in making the change you desire? From my experience, in those situations, the promise of what I desire is so seductive that I can't stop myself from moving forward in faith. In those instances, I just allow myself to be captivated by whatever needs to happen next. I seem to have endless energy to put in the time and work to make it happen.

The difference is not in the type of shifts calling me or the changes I need to make. Instead, I seem to be flooded with love and the promise of possibility and transformation. When I am stuck and unable to heed the shift calling me into action, there seems to be more pain than love, more self-hatred than self-acceptance, and more resistance than allowing. So, pay attention to those times when you are more resistant and judging and to situations where you are more open and allowing your intuition to guide you and the universe to direct you toward greater wholeness.

*What is something concrete you can do to allow the shift calling you to guide you towards more love and wholeness in your life?*

# Forgiveness is Liberating

Forgiveness is allowing a gentle caress, a gentle embrace of love and tenderness, to flow through our being. It allows a release of shame, regret, pain, hurt, anger, or judgment. The healing balm opens the doors for Divine, Universal energy to flow and move freely through our being once again.

It takes a lot of effort to stay resentful. Even if we feel justified in holding on to our anger and truth, we are still using up a large amount of our vital energy to keep our anger and truth in place. I believe we deserve to express our anger. It allows us to release stagnant energy, set clear boundaries, and define our dominion. We also deserve to stand by our truth and express the values that are dear to us. That's what defines our integrity.

But when we don't forgive and stay resentful, we are not releasing our anger or sharing our unique truth. Instead, we are just holding on to the energy and not letting it move through us. So, it festers, requiring us to shut down a precious aspect of our being. Now we have both pent-up energy of resentment, pain, or anger, and we also need to use extra energy to keep all of this stifled within us. That is a lot of energy that we could use for other creative projects in our life.

When we choose to forgive, we allow a considerable amount of pent-up energy to release and become available to use however we choose. When we forgive, we open up the possibility to release our pain, share our anger, and stand up for our truth instead of just keeping it locked up and depleting our vitality. So, forgiving is not about glancing over injustice or emotional wounding. On the contrary, it is about acknowledging it fully, giving it a respectful place, and acknowledging the learning we have gained from this experience. That is how forgiveness becomes a healing balm. It is how it liberates us. And it is how it frees up creative life force for us to use to live more fully.

*When it comes to the shift calling you, what aspect of your situation or part of yourself do you need to forgive and release, and what might be a first and loving step you could take?*

# Your Life is Your Spiritual Practice

There's more to you than meets the eye. Your life is made up of more than the experiences, thoughts, and feelings brought on by your physical existence. You are more than the people and circumstances that have nurtured you into who you are today. You are, first and foremost, a non-physical, spiritual being having an earthly experience. As you might already know, your earthly existence is a small fraction of your full existence. It might not feel this way when the worries of the world bog you down.

This book is all about how to experience yourself more fully as a spiritual being with a unique physical experience. Because you are first and foremost a spiritual being, you can shift into experiencing your life as an ongoing spiritual practice. No longer is your spiritual practice something you do for 20 minutes in the mornings before you go about living a mundane material existence devoid of any meaning and purpose. Instead, your entire life is your spiritual practice, where you can become present to the fullness of your life at any moment throughout your day.

As such, each day offers moments where you can become more of the precious wonder that you are, contributing to the wholeness of your world by living your life to the fullest. For that to happen, you must bring a more expansive and spiritual perspective to your daily interactions and activities. The more you recognize this, the more intentional you can become, exponentially improving your chances for greater meaning and purpose.

The suggestions in this book offer you the tools for a quantum spiritual shift in your perception of yourself and your perspective on life and the world around you. My intention is for them to inspire you to cross the bridge from where you are to where you desire to be.

Using a spiritual lens has helped me grow in many profound ways, personally and professionally. It has helped me be a better parent, spouse, woman, and citizen of planet Earth. As I hear my clients share their struggles and dreams, I listen for the underlying spiritual forces at play. This lens is the most expansive, inclusive, and life-affirming perspective for understanding my life and mentoring those seeking transformation.

As the Expansive Principle is the most important foundation in shifting and transforming your life, I elaborate on it separately in Part IV: Shifting Your Probabilities to Accelerate Your Spiritual Growth. But I want to give it a quick shout-out so that you can familiarize yourself with it.

The Expansive Principle states that when you increase the field of your awareness, you automatically increase the field of information available to you, resulting in more possible solutions. Expanding your consciousness is mostly about creating more spaciousness in your mind, heart, and being. So, it's not about logically figuring out a difficult situation. Instead, it is about surrendering your thinking mind and allowing intuitive wisdom and inner knowing to reveal new possibilities and empowering solutions. When you make expanding your conscious awareness an integral daily practice, you exponentially increase the resources and solutions available to solve your problems.

I'll explain all of this in greater detail in Part IV. For now, I'll say that all the nuggets I share in this book have come from expanding my consciousness and tapping into the wisdom of the Universe. As I talk about in my first book, *Living a Spiritual Life in a Material World*, all spiritual and mystical experiences are expansive in nature. Looking through a spiritual lens, expanding your conscious awareness will increase your capacity to develop your unique path to healing and transformation. At this early stage of the book, I can promise that joy awaits you when you learn to expand your consciousness.

While I believe that our entire life is an ongoing spiritual practice, the area where we spend the most time working is often our spiritual practice on steroids. Pressure turns coal into diamonds. Fire purifies gold. Pain develops purpose. In the material world, we each have an area where challenges seem to concentrate. For some, it's health issues. For others, it's financial challenges. And for others, it's relationships that tend to get the bulk of our energy. We can overcome these challenges and achieve greater harmony by tuning into our spiritual frequency. But we can remain stuck if we ignore the power available to us from spiritual sources.

So, we're back to what's challenging you and what shift is calling you from within. Whatever issue keeps repeating itself in your life, whatever area in your life seems to present you with the most heartache, is the most potent of circumstances for your spiritual growth and transformation. That doesn't mean that you need to suffer to be spiritual. It means you are willing to grow through a particular set of pain points to become a more joyous and whole human being and offer your unique gifts and talents to improve our world.

You have the choice. You can keep unintentionally drawing the same experiences into your life or live with intention and move into a more exciting and empowering life. If you decide to answer the shift calling you and treat your journey of transformation as your spiritual practice, you'll learn necessary spiritual lessons that will bring you profound levels of fulfillment and pure enjoyment, as well as inner freedom balanced with external abundance. You will become a powerful shift-maker in your own life and for those you champion and care for.

We are each here to alleviate our heaviness. By doing so, we alleviate the heaviness of humanity and allow for greater joy, awe, and wonder to fill our lives and the lives of those around us.

***Does it feel overwhelming or liberating to relate to your life as a spiritual practice, and why?***

# Reflection Prompt

While reading this part, I can imagine you've identified at least one shift calling you and demanding your full attention. Once you focus on this issue, take a moment to sit quietly and acknowledge this shift calling. Communicate with this shift calling. Tell it that you are present and willing to show up and befriend it. No more fighting it, blaming it, or rejecting it. This time, you will build a relationship with that which is calling you from within and be willing to make the necessary shifts to experience the change you desire. This time you commit to pouring your love into the challenge or situation you have chosen to focus on until you experience the transformation.

Take a moment to create a concise intention statement. Write a simple, straightforward sentence declaring your deepest desire and your intention. Read your intention to yourself a few times. Take it in and see how it feels. What feelings come up? What critical thoughts creep in? What hopeful thought is encouraging you to heed the shift calling you? Just acknowledge that which is reaching out to you from within.

I've also shared with you what states of being can support your transformation journey and what might be standing in your way of taking action and moving forward. Notice which of these you can most relate to. Then, start paying attention each time it shows up. Notice what you do. Don't judge what you do; just notice it and amplify it when it serves you. If it doesn't, then see if there is anything else you can do to replace this automatic response.

# Part III: The Practice of Shift-Making

*"If you don't know how to fit in this world,*
*it is because you are here to help create a new one."*

—Ajit George

# The Power of Shifting

Are you familiar with the 1 in 60-rule in air navigation? It states that if a pilot shifts the course of a plane by just one degree, which may seem insignificant, after traveling just 60 miles, the plane will be one mile off from its course. The longer the plane flies off course by one degree, the further it will be from its intended path. Yet, the pilot can make a simple mid-flight course correction and reach the desired destination.

Imagine if you could course-correct your life by just one degree. You will surely end up on a different journey than you are currently on and will arrive at a different destination than the one you keep arriving at daily. A compounding effect on whatever track you are on amplifies your thoughts, behaviors, and actions. What you are currently living through is just increasing in the same direction in which it is already going. It keeps you where you are, only more so as you continue on the same track.

Can you imagine where you would end up if you could make a slight course correction, a one-degree shift? What if you could feel more confident in your gifts to the world, less judgmental of yourself, or finally follow through on a project or dream that you have? Can you imagine how this would shift the trajectory of your life? Just thinking of the new possibilities makes me feel happy.

To begin with, it might feel small and even insignificant, but once you've traveled for a while in this new direction, new sceneries will be revealed to you, and new miracles will accompany you along your way to your desired destination. Quantum leaps are initiated by profoundly simple shifts that grow in potency as you keep the momentum going. That's how you ended up where you are today and how you can change the course of your life. Nothing becomes insurmountable when you integrate small shifts into how you think, believe, and act.

That's why, in this book, I suggest making a one-degree course correction by taking each shift at a time and taking your life back in the direction of your desired destination.

*Do you believe that one small shift, compounded over time, can transform your life? If not, what's stopping you from believing it's possible?*

# Shift Before You Change

I've intentionally chosen to name the process of transforming your life, which I lay out in this book, as a "shift" rather than a "change." For me, "shifting" is an internal process where you undergo some modification of your overall mindset and a new awareness of your identity, perspective, and beliefs. It can feel like something is altered emotionally, mentally, spiritually, and even physically. You begin to perceive the world differently, especially when engaging with similar situations as before. You know something significant has shifted in you when you engage within a familiar setting but get new results. You might be surprised how people respond differently to you or new opportunities present themselves. At such times, it seems like you can't go back anymore and see the world like you used to. Your world has transformed. That is what I call a "shift."

The new results you begin to notice and experience are what I call "change." It is the external proof that things are moving in your desired direction. You may begin noticing that you have a different attitude or expectation in a familiar situation and get a different response from the world around you. With your internal shift, you begin to attract new interactions, find yourself in new situations, and realize that you are making different choices and decisions. These are all external manifestations of the change that happens when you shift internally. It is when the internal shifting happens that external changes can begin. Without an internal shift in your awareness, you can push hard for external changes without getting any results, which can be very discouraging. I'm sure you've experienced that many times, without knowing why you could not change your behavior or life circumstance. It can be so discouraging. I've tried it this way myself many times, with little success, only to end up feeling depleted and discouraged.

When you begin by shifting your mind, thoughts, emotions, and relationship with the world around you, magic occurs. You begin to observe external changes and experience the proof you have been waiting and hoping for. So, shifting and changing have a role in your transformation. Start with internal shifting and then experience external changes.

Here are a few examples of internal shifts. It may include shifting your perception of yourself in a more loving and affirming way concerning a particular situation. It can include shifting your perspective on the situation and how you are contributing to the dynamics you are experiencing. And it can include a shift in your attitude and response to the circumstances. The external change will come from your internal shift. The changes will happen because you have made a small

                                                 Shift Calling

but significant inner shift that will change the trajectory of your destination.

*How can you shift from the fixed expectations you may have and instead stay open to new possibilities and unexpected results?*

# Shifts and Quantum Shifts

Some of our decisions may seem small and insignificant, while others may feel life-changing. Whether the shift is big or small, the perspective of time reveals its significance and impact on our lives.

I define shifts as significant choices we make to alter our lives. Quantum shifts occur once we follow through on those initial shifts calling us and discover that nothing is the same anymore. We have shifted our entire identity or perspective, and as a result, our life and world are transformed.

For example, if you choose a new direction in your work, you have to make many incremental decisions before you can sit back and say, *my life does not resemble what it was two years ago*. The decision to leave your previous work situation might have been a big decision, which took you a while to come to, but then you had to make many small internal shifts to grow into your new self. With the perspective of time you realize that this was a quantum shift that has affected your entire life and future, not just your work situation.

The shifts I suggest in this book will help you approach your life circumstances in a whole new way, breathing new life into the shifts calling you. Each suggested shift is first an idea to take in. Then it is a spiritual practice to try out in your daily life and see what happens from this new vantage point. How can you apply it to your particular situation? How can this suggestion help you shift your trajectory, even just by one degree? Then, over a few days, weeks, or months, notice how your inner world is shifting with just this one suggestion. And finally, notice any external changes in your situation. Miracles will accompany you if you allow yourself to receive them.

*Can you recall an area in your life where you experienced the positive effects of shifting over time? What was it like before and after your shifted?*

# Becoming a Shift-Maker

Shifting internally is not a one-time event but an ongoing habit that you get better at the more you practice. Life keeps throwing new challenges at us that we need to deal with. And our list of desires and goals keeps growing as we discover new experiences. For either of these, we need to shift our perception of ourselves and our perspective on the given situation in which we find ourselves, whether circumstantial or chosen. The better we are at the practice of internal shifting to effectuate external change, the quicker we can adjust to the new circumstances we face, whether they are forced upon us or of our choosing. This is a life-long journey; we grow with every step as we improve at shift-making. It is the craft of nurturing our internal and spiritual selves to effectuate external change.

The Transformation Map below illustrates how to practice engaging in incremental shifts with a compounding effect on an ongoing basis. The Transformation Map will help you advance in this book and familiarize yourself with the different principles and suggestions without getting lost or overwhelmed.

It's a simple three-step process, and you can keep using it at any stage. You will want to begin by identifying a shift demanding your full attention. As you review this book and familiarize yourself with the different suggestions, choose one you feel especially drawn to. Then, start practicing it in your daily life. Pay attention to how it shifts your approach to your particular situation. As you keep practicing, notice any immediate benefit. Keep integrating the suggestions in this book to transform your situation and experience greater freedom.

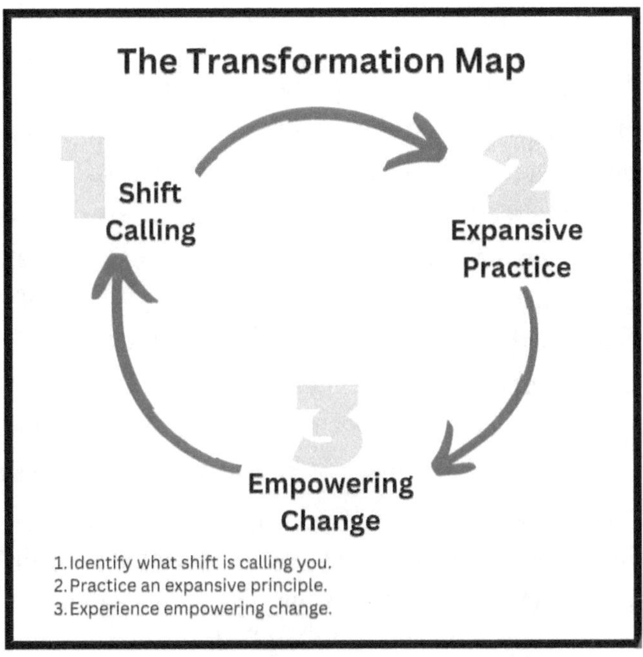


*How does it feel to think of yourself as a shift-maker, and your life as an ongoing practice of shift-making?*

# Shifting is an Act of Love

The expressions "swimming against the current" or "swimming upstream" imply thinking and acting seemingly in opposition to others' expectations. It is associated with putting in more effort while swimming against everyone else's direction. Making a shift can feel like swimming upstream because change can be hard, and shifting your beliefs and habitual thoughts is not easy for anyone. Know that you are not alone in finding it challenging to better your life. You are trying to free your thinking and behavior from the familial and cultural ideologies that got you to where you are in the first place.

First, know that it is not easy. Swimming against an opposing current can be exhausting. The voices telling you that you can't do something can be difficult to fight against. But that's 100 percent okay. It's often a sign you're going the right way. In this case, "going with the flow" may take you away from your desires. Remember, the greatest minds and inventors created life-changing results by going against the norm while envisioning something better for humanity. If they didn't take the risk to swim upstream, where would we all be now?

Second, I'm sure you've experienced that after you've made a significant shift in how you value yourself and traded a bad habit for a life-affirming one, you have to stop hanging out with people who feel more toxic than supportive. You might feel like you are betraying people dear to you but find that you can no longer betray yourself. It can feel like you are swimming against the current, yet you can't go back. You have come to value yourself more than staying around the people who put you down or compel you to engage in self-destructive behavior. Just because they are familiar doesn't mean they're better for you or can help you achieve your deepest desires. Loneliness can become solitude. Finding uplifting friends can bring you closer to what you desire.

I want to offer you an expansive, life-affirming, and purpose-filled reframe of how to relate to swimming against the current. Think of salmon, who, after spending their adult life swimming in the oceans, head back home to the Source from where they came. They are heading back to the stream where they were born to lay eggs and offer themselves as food for the next generation. They are not struggling to swim upstream; they are just called to return home and obey this inner calling. While on one level, this can be described as a biological instinct, on a spiritual plane, it is an act of devotion and sacrifice of the highest order—an act of love. Like the salmon, we are each called to return to our source, and the shift calling us is the invitation and our portal to find our way back home to our source. Thinking of this always moves me and connects me to a deep sense of a higher purpose, a sacred intention driven by Divine Love to fulfill my life's purpose and serve the world.

Can you recall a time in your life when you experienced feeling like you were swimming against the current? When we go against our parents, partners, friends, and the mainstream culture, it can feel like swimming against the current. If you recall such a time in your life, you probably also remember it felt like you had no choice but to follow your heart or dreams, even if it meant letting go of the familiar and feeling out of your comfort zone. Such moments are a call from your inner being, your soul, guiding you towards greater love, joy, creativity, and wholeness.

From this noble perspective, your shifts are always an act of deep love for yourself and your world. When you make a significant shift in your life from such a place of love, then the heaviness of swimming upstream is lifted. Instead, you get to experience awakening to your true nature and life purpose.

You have the opportunity to be reminded of your preciousness and the preciousness of life. Suddenly, the desire to become your best awakens in you because you feel part of something bigger, which gives you a sense of purpose. You are not struggling alone anymore. Rather, you are engaged in the process of swimming upstream, back home to your essence. And when you are closer to living from your essence, the world becomes a better place for all of us.

*Is there anything you'd be willing to swim against the current to make happen?*

# Spiritual Work is World Work

When I began homeschooling my children, as I shared earlier, I did it because of very personal circumstances. The local municipality didn't allow us to send my older son, who was six at the time, to the public school of our choice because of local internal politics at the county level. As my son was not enjoying school within a few weeks of starting and would ask to stay home a few days a week, my immediate need was to find a viable solution for him, which is how I found myself, unexpectedly, homeschooling. At the time, I had no grand philosophical opinions about the best education for children. I was just desperate to stop my son's misery.

As I began familiarizing myself with homeschooling practices I got more comfortable as the primary educator of my children. I began feeling that I was not just dealing with the different daily activities with which we were engaged, like swimming lessons, crafts, reading and writing, or going to the neighborhood playground. I also began feeling there was a bigger purpose at play, and that gave me a great sense of purposefulness. I felt I was an activist, a change-maker, acting locally at the level of my immediate family's needs but thinking globally at the level of educating the next generation.

I had a doctorate in transformative learning, and my professional and private life began merging. I created a holistic education model that we used as our framework for homeschooling. I began feeling that my life purpose and family circumstances were coming together, which gave me a greater sense of purpose. It motivated me to become a better homeschooling parent. And I felt I was at the frontline of education, like the renowned Swiss child psychologist Piaget, who developed his theory of cognitive child development from observing his own children.

In my unique case, many pieces of my life came together at this juncture. I could give my children the best education I believed I could give them. Homeschooling also became my second chance to heal from my childhood traumas in the public school system. And my professional life as an educator was inspired by educating my children. Our daily activities as a family became learning opportunities for my children and me as an educator developing a holistic theory of education. You cannot imagine the joy I experienced waking up every morning. I'd go to sleep tired every night from the full days of being with my kids all the time. But I'd wake up every morning with renewed excitement to start another day and a new adventure.

While healing my childhood wounds, giving my children a great education, and developing professionally, I felt I was doing personal, spiritual, and world work. I was a shift-maker, shifting internally in great leaps, as well as a change-maker, consciously effectuating social change with these two precious little beings who were put in my custody to raise to the best of my capacity. My soul was in heaven as my spirit soared.

While most people's shifts don't involve homeschooling and developing an original education model, we each have shifts waiting for us to show up and do the work to become fully aligned with our highest, most enlightened selves. In doing so, we help alleviate the heaviness of humanity and increase the probability of humankind becoming its most enlightened self.

This can happen when you undergo internal shifts and allow the universe to change your external circumstances. You will realize that the thing that has plagued you for so long is your ultimate liberation. Many aspects of your life will begin coming together in such perfect unison that you can only feel deep joy and contentment. I believe that when you bring together personal, spiritual, and world work, you find the perfect balance between self-actualizing and living a purpose-filled life of service. This is not "sacrificing" yourself in service to others. Instead, you make our world a better place by living the full life you are capable of living.

In sports, until someone breaks a world record, everyone believes it is not possible to break that particular record. But when someone finally does, suddenly, many others can break that same record. An internal shift of identity and perspective happens within that community of athletes. Suddenly, they all believe it's possible to break that world record and that they can be one of those people. The same is true in our individual worlds and the people we touch, locally or globally. We uplift each other and make each other better.

If you have been primarily focused on inner personal work or making internal shifts, then I invite you, as you work through this book, to expand your identity into both a shift-maker and a change-maker. When we see our personal and spiritual work as world work—as uplifting humanity—we offer others insight into what is possible for them because it is possible for us.

Alternatively, if you identify primarily as a change-maker, a social, political, or ecological activist, then I invite you to expand your perception of yourself as becoming a shift-maker committed to personal growth so that you may become more effective in your world work.

Here's my invitation to you, whether you have a greater affinity with personal work, spiritual work, or world work:

> *Join the spiritual evolution!*
> *Do your personal work and treat*
> *it like a spiritual practice.*
> *Together, as a global village, we can*
> *uplift humanity and our planet.*

You don't need to know exactly how your inner work will also serve as world work, or vice versa. Open yourself up to the possibility that the two are related and influence each other. Know that integrating personal and spiritual work with world work will give you a renewed sense of purpose and make effectuating any change, whether personal or world-centered, less heavy and challenging. It will feel less like swimming upstream against the current and more like coming home to your most enlightened self. I believe that at this time in history, we need people like you to change your destiny and that of humanity and our planet. I invite you to accompany me on this spiritual journey, heeding the shift that's calling you to change. It promises to be an expansive journey where you will be invited to experience yourself and perceive the world from a more inclusive, life-affirming, and wondrous viewpoint. May you find new ways to shift internally so that you can access empowering creative solutions that will deepen your love for yourself and our world. Let's begin with shifting your probabilities to accelerate your spiritual growth.

*Does it feel intimidating or empowering to think of your personal work as world work, and why?*

# Reflection Prompt

Now you know that shifting one degree consistently will have a compounding effect on your trajectory and desired destination. So, you can practice by shifting one small thing in your daily routine and see what effect it has on your day, mood, attitude, and interactions with other people. I offer you different shifts of a spiritual nature throughout this book but try first to make a shift of your own and observe what happens. See if you can sustain the shift or whether you fall back into habitual behavior. Inquire about what stops you from sustaining your internal shift. See whether it is easier to sustain your shift if you see it as an act of self-love. Observe whether your dedication to making a one-degree shift changes when you consider it your spiritual practice or serving the greater good.

# Part IV: Shifting Your Probabilities to Accelerate Your Spiritual Growth

*"As human beings we are made to surpass ourselves*
*and are truly ourselves only when*
*transcending ourselves."*

—Huston Smith

# Shifting to a Higher Altitude

In chapter three of my book, *Living a Spiritual Life in a Material World*, I compare being in a spiritual state to rising above turbulence when flying a plane and finding a higher altitude where there is less turbulence, and the atmosphere is calm. I explain that spirituality is all about "rising to a higher altitude of emotional and mental stability where there is no turbulence and your being can sail over the disturbances of daily life with greater ease." This doesn't mean that if you are spiritual, you don't have challenges in your life. It just means you can face them with greater perspective, a more resilient attitude, and a more efficient and effective set of tools. It means you can deal with the shift calling you from an elevated perspective, a more expansive view of the situation, which will help you discover a more self-affirming and favorable path toward a significant change and meaningful transformation.

In contrast, often, when we deal with our daily human problems, we get bogged down and caught up in emotional turmoil. We forget that we are spiritual beings having an earthly experience and instead think of ourselves as human beings who, every now and then, have a spiritual experience. In doing so, we shut ourselves off from the vital flow of Source energy, which can keep us connected to a more meaningful, purposeful, and joy-filled existence. As a result, we often feel that we are in a constant battle with everything coming at us from all directions—at home, at work, and in the world. And we miss out on the life-affirming and creative solutions that come with being connected to Source and the wholeness of life.

In that same chapter of my book, I continue to say that "what separates you and me from mystics, prophets, and sages is that they naturally reside for long periods of time in this expansive spiritual altitude and therefore have access to higher, otherworldly truths that can transform our earthly existence." But such luminaries were not born this way. They might be innately drawn to spiritual states and exploration, but they have often studied with a teacher and followed some particular rigorous practice. We each have the capacity to grow, attain higher spiritual states, and benefit from higher wisdom to solve our personal and collective challenges. It is my belief and experience that we don't need to undergo rigorous practice to attain such levels. We just need to consistently integrate higher states of consciousness into our daily lives. As Lao Tzu suggests, "The key to growth is the introduction of higher dimensions of consciousness into our awareness."

Doing this can accelerate our spiritual growth and increase our probability of significant transformation, leading to more joy and fulfillment. That's why I've borrowed the term "probabilities" from mathematics, as it describes so well the increase

                              Shift Calling

in chances for success using the suggestions I offer in this part of the book. While I can imagine that the shift calling you is probably of an earthy human nature, by understanding fundamental spiritual truths, you will acquire tools to gain greater perspective for altering your course en route to a desired destination.

It is also important to remember that transformation is not an end goal but rather an ongoing way of life. So, to increase your probability for significant ongoing transformation and to make this your unique and creative journey, I answer vital questions in this part of the book, such as the purpose and meaning of life. I also address universal principles that are the foundation for the applications I share in later parts of the book, which you can apply to your unique life circumstances.

*From your experience, what does it feel like when you are able to rise to a higher emotional attitude when dealing with challenges?*

# The Substance of Life

Spiritual traditions, holistic healing modalities, and quantum physics all point to the fact that everything in the universe is made up of energy in different forms and degrees of density, some physical and some non-physical. This energy that makes up the universe vibrates at a different frequency depending on the unique properties of each entity or species. This rule is true for everything physical on planet Earth, humans, animals, plants, and minerals, as well as for all the artifacts we've created as part of our civilization. And it is also true of non-physical forms of energy, ranging from our thoughts and emotions to great beings whom we may contact through telepathy. These beings include angels, deceased luminaries, our loved ones who have transitioned, or beings from other planets.

All these existing forms of energy, physical and non-physical, have consciousness. Now, when I talk about consciousness, I hold it to consist of four elements: 1) A defined identity or field, 2) with innate intelligence, 3) unique capabilities, and 4) an awareness, on some level, of itself. That is the basis of our universe—consciousness forming, evolving, and manifesting. These four elements hold true for all levels of existence.

To make this more tangible, imagine a single cell in your body. It has a defined form with an innate intelligence to perform specific functions, using unique capabilities and awareness of itself as an aspect of creation. When combined with many other cells, this one cell creates elaborate organic systems with higher levels of complexity and more elaborate levels of conscious intelligence. A pebble in a river is made of minerals. Minerals exist throughout the cosmos at different levels of formation. From this perspective, the mineral kingdom is a vast conscious intelligence essential to our planet's existence. Think of atoms of oxygen that come together to provide the conditions for life on Earth and the trees that convert carbon dioxide into oxygen for us to breathe.

From this vantage point, imagine yourself as part of the human species, the creative force on planet Earth. We are beings of great complexity and conscious awareness, able to imagine and use tools to bring into being what we are imagining. We are beings who have access to consciousness both in its non-physical form of thought and imagination, as well as in the physical, material expression of consciousness, through the lives we live and the civilization we have built. In addition, we can self-reflect and change the course of our attitude, our perception, and our actions, because we have been given free will and the capacity to choose. Pretty magical, wouldn't you say?

These are all evidence of a glorious, intelligent universe where everything is consciousness. And this consciousness manifests, at different times, to varying degrees of density, which we often categorize as either physical or non-physical. This is an ongoing process of evolution—but not just a physical evolution. It's an evolution of consciousness, expressed in physical and non-physical ways throughout the universe.

It may feel a bit abstract to imagine everything in our universe as fields of intelligent energy interacting with each other to form our universe. Still, it is worthwhile to try on this perspective and sense how it may allow us a more expansive sense of ourselves and our world. It can help take away some of the stories we tell ourselves about the world, which may limit our understanding of the true nature of reality and our life and place in this vast universe. And it can offer a renewed and more empowered approach to dealing with our lives.

We share this capacity to be conscious with all humans. Yet, we bring our individual, unique identity, with its innate intelligence, our unique capabilities, and the capacity to be aware of ourselves and the world around us. This is how complex and incredibly designed we are.

Imagine approaching the unique ailments you face in your daily life from this vantage point where everything has conscious awareness. Can you imagine dialoguing with a particular part of your body as a conscious field that can offer you vital insight into your health and well-being? We may call this intuition or our subconscious communicating with us. Either way, the different parts of our body are conscious and alive and can give us information about how to heal ourselves or increase our well-being. The same is true for every aspect of our world. It is conscious and alive. All we have to do is begin communicating and co-creating a better world for ourselves and others.

*Which part of the shift calling you would you like to begin dialoguing with as if it was fully alive and could give you answers? What would be your opening question?*

# The Purpose of Life

Throughout the ages, many have tried to figure out the purpose of our existence, from the great philosophers who spent their life contemplating this question to you and me, who have probably asked ourselves this question many times during a challenging moment. While on one level, we each have unique life stories and, therefore, unique life purposes, there is also a collective purpose to creation and life on planet Earth. I'm bringing this up here so that you can connect more fully to what you have to offer the world and, as a result, live with greater intention, express yourself more fully, and find greater meaning and significance in the events in your life.

Remember I said in Part II, What Shift is Calling You? that desire is required to begin a shift? Well, knowing the purpose of life and how you might express this purpose uniquely might just awaken in you a passionate desire to initiate a significant shift. And if we each engage in a significant shift aligned with the purpose of life itself, then humanity and all life on planet Earth will be uplifted.

This is my answer to the fundamental question humans have been asking themselves throughout the ages: "What is the purpose of life?"

*The purpose of life is to experience itself.*

That's right. On all levels of existence, consciousness wants to experience itself, in whatever form it exists, from a single cell in your body and the different complex systems that keep you alive to all the non-physical aspects of your being and the span of your life. At each level, from an atom we can't see with our bare eye to the complexity of your soul's unique journey in this lifetime, the purpose of each component that makes up *YOU* is to experience itself. The cells that make up your muscles desire to experience their capabilities of strength and mobility. Only when they do that can they fulfill the purpose for which they were created. Likewise, your soul desires to experience your unique and precious capabilities as a loving, creative human being with the power to choose how you want to live and the capacity to create the life you want for yourself.

For the cells in your muscular system to experience themselves, they must express themselves fully. The same is true for the whole of you. To experience yourself fully, you have to express your unique self fully. Otherwise, you will not be able to experience your unique soul and personality to the fullest. So, your muscles need you to use them to express the purpose for which they were created and to experience the full range of their capacity. And expressing yourself fully, in all dimensions and areas of your life, is a prerequisite to experiencing yourself fully. Suppose you don't express the full range of your physical abilities, emotional dimensions, mental agility, and spiritual competencies. In that case, you cannot fully experience the purpose for which you exist and are alive, in your body temple, in this lifetime.

Life experiencing itself through us experiencing ourselves is confirmation of our existence. I experience myself; therefore, I exist. I experience myself fully, and therefore, I am fully engaged with my life and the world.

The shifts calling us are those places where we are not experiencing our full capabilities. Those are the places where something is stuck, where there is something to explore, something new to learn and better understand. By doing so, we attain new levels of conscious awareness and freedom of expression.

It's important to realize that it is a process, not a one-time goal. It's a lifestyle to keep heeding the next shift calling so that we can become our fullest selves and experience ourselves in even more wondrous, creative, and loving ways. It is the craft of shift-making and what makes us shift-makers, as we keep making internal shifts that produce external changes.

A simple image that might help illustrate this is looking at toddlers master their walking. Have you seen how proud they feel for standing up straight, keeping their balance, and walking from where they are to the table on the other side of the room? They seem as engaged in exploring the range of their capabilities in all the previous attempts when they fell and had to get up again. And, yet, as they build their muscles and stabilize themselves a bit more, they reach the moment when they reach that table or walk into their parents' arms. Having mastered this, they can continue to the next shift and level. Toddlers naturally encounter the world surrounding them by engaging with their physical capabilities. They experience themselves more fully by constantly shifting their perception of what they are capable of doing. They experience the world as their playground.

The magic begins when all parts of creation express themselves fully and interact in a co-creative, interconnected whole. That takes the purpose of life to the next level—transforming itself and creating itself anew. In experiencing yourself, you learn, grow, and change—evolving your consciousness and physical reality. You can choose what beliefs you want to hold on to and which you wish to let go of and replace with other, more life-affirming, loving, and empowering beliefs. You can choose which relationships you wish to keep nurturing and which are too toxic. You can choose dreams you want to make real in this lifetime. You can begin to trust when a shift is calling you from within as you realize that life is asking to experience itself through you more fully. And you accept the call to take your life to the next level and experience yourself even more fully.

***In your particular life circumstances, how is it helpful for you to know that the purpose of life is to experience itself?***

# The Meaning of Life

The meaning of life is both very personal and universal. What brings you meaning will differ from what brings me meaning. It would depend on what you love and care for, your values, and your beliefs. And that's very personal. But we all share that what brings us meaning is what we love and care for, what we value and hold as precious and noble—that which makes us come alive, expressing our passion, our gifts, and our talents with joy. In fact, experiencing and feeling any spiritual quality or principle will bring you a deep sense of meaning—this includes watching someone you care for succeed, expressing your gifts and talents and being acknowledged and appreciated for them, and feeling part of a group that champions a cause that is dear to you.

There are endless examples of what would give your life meaning. They are all expressions of love, self-love, love for one another, awe, wonder, and witnessing the glory of life. If you look deeply into what gives your life meaning, you will find that it is a derivative of any of these examples. Meaning comes from taking in the magnificence of it all, and yet, we each make meaning in ways that are uniquely creative and heart-opening to us.

Then there is the larger meaning of our life on planet Earth, which I think is important to be aware of, as it can help us move from feeling isolated to feeling that we are part of something greater and that our life matters. You see, I believe that life on planet Earth is a cosmic experiment, and we are all part of this experiment, living on the edge of creation.

On planet Earth, everything is created separate, at least on the physical plane. Each tree is separate, each animal is distinct, and each human is unique. Even each snowflake is particular. So, we come into this world as separate individual human beings, in addition to being given free will and the power to choose. Humans are also the creative force on our planet, with the ability to imagine something and create it in physical form. So, we have access to both the spiritual and the material world, the non-physical and the physical. That gives us unique creative powers.

As a result, I believe the cosmic experiment of planet Earth is about creating a magnificent physical world born out of a consciousness of magnificence and a world of love and beauty created out of a consciousness of love and beauty. The possibilities are endless, but they all lead to variations of creative wonder and an appreciation for the glory of creation. The mission is to create a physical world that manifests the glory of Divine Consciousness and remain connected to this Divine Consciousness as we live a physical life that is defined by individuation.

This is the experiment that we are part of. And you and I, and all of humanity, being the creative force on this planet, are here at the edge of creation, experimenting with staying connected to the sacredness, sentience, and preciousness of life while experimenting with expressing ourselves as separate individuals. The process will look different for each one of us, and yet it will all come together into a divine harmony. So you see, the meaning of life has universal qualities which will be expressed uniquely through each of us.

We are all living on the edge of creation, using our free will to choose how we live and what we create. As the purpose of life is to experience ourselves and our world to the fullest, we get to do just that in each moment. The result is ongoing transformation. As we experiment with new ways of doing habitual things and new attitudes to apply to familiar situations, we shift internally, change our external circumstances, and experience our ongoing transformation.

The three questions to ask yourself if you want more meaning in your life are:

*How can I live on the edge of creation each day*
*so that I can experience the transformations I desire?*

*How can I keep my connection to Source flowing*
*while I experience physical separation?*

*How can I create my life and influence my*
*world in a manner that expresses*
*my ongoing connection to Divine*
*Consciousness, to God, to Source?*

**What meaningful and sacred opportunities open up for you regarding the shift calling you to transform?**

# The Expansive Principle

The three principles I'm about to share with you build on each other like building blocks. The Expansive Principle is the first and most significant, as it informs everything else and is the key to accelerating your spiritual growth. It is the basis for any internal shifting and external change and, therefore, is at the core of your personal growth and spiritual illumination. So let's examine the principle further.

The Expansive Principle states that when you increase the field of your awareness, you automatically increase the field of information available to you, resulting in more possible solutions. Expanding your consciousness is mostly about creating more spaciousness in your mind, heart, and being. It's not about logically figuring out a difficult situation. Instead, it is about surrendering your thinking mind and allowing intuitive wisdom and inner knowing to reveal new possibilities and empowering solutions. So, when you make expanding your conscious awareness an integral daily practice, you exponentially increase the resources and solutions available to you.

While the concept of the Expansive Principle might be new to you, I am sure you have experienced it inadvertently before. For example, it's a state of mind often experienced when you feel relaxed. Your breath is deep, calm, and steady. You may recall a time like this when you started to feel detached from whatever might have preoccupied your attention. You may have felt gratitude, enjoyment, love, and even bliss. New thoughts opened up, which seemed to be wiser and more creative. It is an overall life-affirming experience that injects vitality and renewed care for ourselves, others, and everything we encounter.

I first came across the Expansive Principle during my doctoral research when I discovered that all spiritual experiences have an expansive quality to them, and the more mystical or transcendent the experience, the greater the sense of expansion. What I have experienced personally, and observed in others, is that during such moments, we experience one, or all three, of the following distinctive qualities: 1) a deep sense of relaxation; 2) an emotional feeling of appreciation, love, or bliss; and 3) a mental awareness of a larger field of information, which did not seem to be available prior to this sense of expansion.

For example, as you breathe deeply, you are expanding the range of your breath. When you feel more loving and compassionate, you expand your emotional palette to be more understanding and forgiving of yourself and others. When you have thoughts that seem to come from a wise inner source or have creative ideas pop into your head, you have expanded the options available to you. Consequently, the more you understand yourself and others, the more you spread understanding in the world. The kinder you are to yourself and others, the more kindness you help spread around you. The more creative you are, the more creativity you share with those in your sphere. What you embody and share expands and ripples out into the world.

Expansive states often bring a sense of physical spaciousness. You may sense that your physical boundaries become more fluid and blend with your surroundings. It is easy to get a sense of this sensation when you spend time in nature and take in its vastness and beauty.

During such moments of "expansive presence," your emotions become more loving and life-affirming. You become more compassionate and caring. You often feel more grateful for your life. In addition, you can often see a purpose running through your life and get a perspective on how all the events in your life have led you to this particular moment. You feel that you are not alone but part of something greater. You are able to reframe more easily the challenging experiences in your life and access appreciation for what you've learned about yourself and others. You can expand your ability to let go of resentments, take responsibility and ultimately forgive yourself and others.

When you expand your presence, you open yourself up to more possibilities and solutions than you had available when your awareness was more constricted. It's the difference between getting around with your GPS on your mobile phone and looking at the map as a whole. The GPS offers turn-by-turn directions, whereas looking at the entire map of the city or the region allows you to perceive many possible routes to your destination. Maybe you have errands to do on the way, or you prefer the scenic route and taking a hike to get your daily exercise in. The point is that you get a more expansive view of your options and can therefore develop more creative and inclusive solutions.

The Expansive Principle directs your attention to a larger context for your life, including its current external circumstances, your life purpose and trajectory, and many more considerations of which you are not even aware. When you expand your consciousness, you expand what becomes available to you through your intuitive and active senses. And so, you may have a sudden insight that seems to come out of nowhere. This insight often feels like the perfect solution for your situation, and you may even wonder why you didn't think of it before.

The ultimate expansion is one where your individual self, as you know it, experiences union with all life. At such times, you feel you are as large as the cosmos and small as a grain of sand. Everything you focus on becomes an intricate part of who you are as you expand your awareness to include what seemed, until now, to be out there, not a part of you. Instead, it is now an intimate part of who you are. This phenomenon is accompanied by a sense of wholeness, peacefulness, and compassion, for you no longer feel isolated and alone. Instead, you feel that you are part of something bigger and greater, and the suffering or thriving of others, human, animal, plant, or mineral, becomes your suffering and your thriving.

In addition, the more you expand your horizon to include more and more parts of the world into your being, the less you feel attached to a specific outcome. The less you seem to care about things happening your way, the more understanding you become of other ways of thinking and living, which may initially seem foreign to you. And that, in turn, increases your sense of joy, capacity to experience loving kindness, and creative expression. You can see how intentionally practicing expanding your consciousness can bring more understanding and peace into our world.

When a shift calls you from within, a part of you is constricted, contracted, and stuck. It is that part of you feeling unappreciated, unloved, and even self-hating. Releasing that trapped energy, which is often accompanied by difficult life stories and trauma, will expand the vital energy accessible to you, allowing you to access greater levels of expansion, which will translate into greater degrees of compassion, under-standing, and love for yourself and others. So, you can see how important the Expansive Principle is to your healing, growth, and transformation.

Simply put, the Expansive Principle is about becoming a larger, more expanded version of yourself, expanding upon your perception of yourself, your perspective on life, and the probabilities for success and happiness. Through expansion, you have more to offer the world. For example, if you see your-self as a more precious, loving, beautiful soul, kinder, or more enthusiastic and grateful, the Expansive Principle is at work. If you believe in yourself more than ever before, then you have allowed the Expansive Principle to increase your belief in your-self. If you are able to expand the scope, the reach, or the depth of your work and life calling, then it is due to the Expansive Principle, which allows you to keep expanding endlessly, both internally and externally. You might not think of it as you go about your daily living. Still, you may notice deeper, more meaningful relationships and experiences due to allowing the Expansive Principle to work through you.

We often work against the natural laws of the universe and block ourselves from expanding into greater and greater levels of awareness. So, whatever shift is calling you from within, it is a call to move toward a more whole and life-affirming version of yourself.

Like many of the concepts in this book, the Expansive Principle is profoundly simple, meaning it is easy to understand and even practice, yet its implications are far-reaching. For example, when you perceive yourself as a spiritual being and a rational, thinking being, you have expanded the scope of your perception of yourself. Perceiving yourself as a spiritual being is not just an idea that you intellectually understand but a new way of being in the world and relating to yourself and others. Practiced over time, you can imagine how you will expand physically, emotionally, mentally, and spiritually from such a new understanding of yourself. This will affect everything you do, your interactions, your decisions, and, of course, the tangible results.

Start paying attention to the Expansive Principle at work throughout your day. It's like noticing gravity's prevalence because the Expansive Principle is always available. The Expansive Principle constantly strives toward greater wholeness in your life and our world. Pay attention to how it shows up in your life, inviting you to meet all its expansive opportunities.

*What might be your favorite way to expand your conscious awareness so you can experience more spaciousness and ease with your particular situation?*

# The Principle of
# Spiritual-Material Wholeness

As I practiced expanding my consciousness over the years, I began to perceive a more inclusive view of the nature of reality, such as discovering the Principle of Spiritual-Material Wholeness. This principle became evident when I visited a friend in the English countryside. She lived in the middle of lush green fields with wildflowers and hills covered with trees in dark green hues. One morning, I woke up and raised my head, looking out at the beautiful fields and hills in the distance. Clouds in the sky provided a beautiful backdrop, a gray contrast to the green of the hills. As I lay there looking out, I felt my heart expanding with an appreciation for the beauty I saw. This appreciation spilled over to feeling grateful for my life in general. I was filled with a deep sense of joy and connection to everything.

Then in this expansive blissful state, I had a profound realization. Nature is in perfect spiritual-material unity. The fields of grass and the trees' trunks, branches, and foliage were the material expressions of nature. But nature also expressed what we would categorize as spiritual qualities, such as peacefulness and beauty. Nature was expressing these spiritual qualities through its physical manifestation. The flowers in the field were expressions of joy and beauty, and the cloud formations above were expressions of serenity and spaciousness. I had never thought of nature as "spiritual," although I had enjoyed the many qualities I felt in its presence.

It made me realize that the physical form of different plants, their shape, color, and scent, served to awaken us to the myriad of human emotions and spiritual presence. Everything is consciousness, and trees and flowers are an expression of consciousness as well. They emanate spiritual qualities, which are part of their unique composition and manifestation, like velvety red petals, lush green leaves, or a sweet fragrance. While some of us love roses while others prefer dahlias, flowers are a material manifestation of the joy and beauty in our world. As such, they can serve as a portal to joy and beauty for us humans because when we are connected to those qualities, we can perceive them in everything around us. We find joy in the people we meet and beauty in our surroundings and ourselves. We become more appreciative of our world and, as a result, we act more kindly toward ourselves and others. As joy and beauty connect us to a greater sense of meaning and the sacredness of our life, we can extend these quality to others.

As I lay there considering nature was in perfect spiritual-material unity, I realized that as humans are part of nature, we, too, are an expression of spiritual-material wholeness. We are physical and spiritual beings who can express our spiritual nature in our daily material life. When you meditate and feel peacefulness, you experience this peacefulness in your body and being. You sense the physical expression of the peacefulness that you experienced during meditation. If you can keep connected to this peacefulness, you become a living, walking, talking expression of peacefulness. You have created a field of peace within your being, which you now emanate, and which will affect your interactions, your choices and decisions, and the results of your actions in the world. The same goes for any quality you are experiencing, be it enthusiasm, delight, playfulness, caring, or grieving. You become a physical expression of these spiritual and emotional qualities. You become an expression and a conduit of them in our physical, material world.

The Principle of Spiritual-Material Wholeness is also present in your environment and all the objects you use and interact with throughout your day. The books you read contain big ideas, words of wisdom, or a captivating story in the form of ink on paper. When you read the book, it transforms again into your imagination or your insight and gleaned wisdom.

Your smartphone, which many would say has no spiritual value, is a portal to ideas worth spreading, remedies to heal an ailment, and connection with family and friends. These are all valuable possibilities that your smartphone offers you. So, if you value family connection or uplifting music, your smartphone is not just a material icon of no emotional and spiritual value. Instead, it is a means to experience and connect, uplifting your spirit and serving as a portal to inspiration.

If, on the other hand, you ignore the spiritual-material wholeness of your existence, then you miss out on all the magic that exists in our world. You don't perceive miracles when they abound in your life, and you don't create magic throughout your day. In fact, you end up contributing to the heaviness in the world because you don't treat your work as a sacred expression of your unique gifts and talents. You don't imbue the material products you produce, the services you offer, and your interactions with others as material expressions of the vibrant spiritual and emotional dimensions of your existence. And then you wonder why you feel so depleted from the daily grind and feel the weight and heaviness in the world.

There is a wholeness of spirit and matter, of the physical and non-physical dimensions of existence on planet Earth. You have the choice and agency to become a conscious creator of the spiritual world you wish to manifest in your material existence. You can engage in a physical environment that nourishes you and reminds you of your spiritual essence. You can practice experiencing the Principle of Spiritual-Material Wholeness by looking for spiritual qualities hidden within and around you, in material objects you interact with daily.

For example, if you want to intentionally spread certain spiritual qualities to your surroundings and interactions, then decide on a quality you would like to practice first. Imagine yourself as a physical portal or conduit of this quality in everything you do. Imagine yourself, for example, as a walking field of ease, care, self-empowerment, enjoyment, or curiosity. Remember that you are the material expression of these qualities, a potent field that influences that which you encounter. You can practice a different spiritual quality each day or stick with one for a longer time and get to know it more intimately.

You can also use the physical world around you to connect with spiritual qualities, becoming the recipient of spiritual-material wholeness. You can go to a particular park that connects you to tranquility and sit there for a while, taking in the different elements that inspire tranquility in you. You could eat a meal that connects you to nourishment and take the time to feel deeply satiated in your body and soul. And you could read the words from a particular book and acknowledge how the ideas inspire you to become an unstoppable force, which could motivate you in your next creative project.

In all of these examples, whether you are the instigator or the recipient of spiritual-material wholeness, remember that by being aware of both levels, you deepen the meaning of each experience and make it more alive and purposeful. By tapping into this spiritual-material principle, I hope you can see how this single concept has the power and probability to accelerate your spiritual growth, and transform your life and your world.

***How can you benefit from applying the Principle of Spiritual-Material Wholeness to the particular shift calling you?***

# The Principle of Physical and Non-Physical Synergy

One of the teachings that most intrigued me when I had my spiritual budding at the Findhorn Foundation in Northern Scotland in my early forties is that nature has a consciousness with which we can interact and collaborate. Specifically, Dorothy Maclean, who I mention earlier in the book, was known for communicating with the consciousness aspect of different plants and elements of nature. She did so when a community member needed simple gardening advice, as well as to better understand the nature of reality and how humanity could live in greater harmony with nature. Through meditation, Dorothy would expand her consciousness and find connection with nature in the shared inner worlds. She received messages from what she called Devas, the consciousness that holds the pattern of each plant species in the spiritual realms, like the pea garden, the daisy, or the oak tree. Through this connection, she and, later on, other community members learned how to connect to the sacredness within everything and themselves.

The practical gardening advice they received through daily meditations from the consciousness of nature allowed them to grow magnificent gardens in barren sandy soil, which became world-famous for being a seemingly supernatural phenomenon. They received practical messages about how to make the soil richer and more fertile for planting, what distance to plant different plants, and how to keep bugs from eating up plants without using pesticides. The messages included practical gardening tips and how to use their focused consciousness to improve their garden. They also received messages about how to become more loving, conscious, and evolved human beings. They never intended to be gardeners or to found a world-renowned community. They just attuned to the inner spiritual dimension of the plants and elements of nature through focused meditation and received valuable advice about gardening and evolving the consciousness of humanity and planet Earth.

That's where I first discovered the Principle of Physical and Non-Physical Synergy, a term I coined based on my observations of the incredible results of humans collaborating with the non-physical, higher consciousness of nature to grow vegetables, fruit, and flowers in great harmony. I found it so very exciting to realize that the world was fully alive and that I could have an inner, telepathic conversation with a particular tree or flower species and, in fact, any element of nature. I have come to know this as a sacred collaboration of the highest intention, where a creative synergy occurs between life's physical and non-physical dimensions.

This collaborative synergy between the physical and non-physical realms is more common than we think. For example, I have a friend who is a poet and a painter. When she sits down to write a poem inspired by one of her paintings, she invites her inner council of poets to join her and inspire her in the process. Whether these are dead or alive poets, she takes a moment to feel into each one of them, their personality, talent, and unique writing. My friend elevates her poetic capabilities by tapping into the inspiring wisdom of well-known and talented poets. This type of communication is available to all of us who want to collaborate with forces in our world that can be accessed through internal meditation and focus.

Another example, which you might be familiar with, is Napoleon Hill's famous "Invisible Counselors," which he describes in his seminal book *Think and Grow Rich*. Hill picked famous people who he admired for their successful endeavors. He would connect with each of them daily, asking them to impart their wisdom and knowledge to him to build his character for greater success. The now well-known formula of a mastermind group was first conceived out of Hill's daily practice. It is based on the idea that when two or more people come together in a shared focus, a group mind develops wiser than the sum of the participants present, offering a larger field of creative solutions.

On a more personal note, this book has taken on a life of its own in much the same way. I knew from the start what I wanted to write about, but as I have gotten deeper into the writing process, I find myself being directed to stop, sometimes for weeks, to process something I am working on. I find myself needing to do some personal work to shift my perspective or perception of myself. When I return to my writing, I feel guided to communicate with you in a new way I had not originally intended. New and deeper layers of the ideas I had originally planned are revealed to me, each in its own timing. As a result, I feel that I am both the writer of this book and its steward. I am serving this book and its message. I am putting in the time and resources to make it as accessible as possible to you, the reader, but the book guides me toward what will serve our world and the evolution of consciousness on our planet. It is very much a physical and non-physical synergy.

Here is how I understand this Principle of Physical and Non-Physical Synergy and how you can use it to benefit your life and your world. As I described in the chapter The Meaning of Life, we mostly experience ourselves and everything in the world as uniquely separate. But when we can tap into the wholeness and interconnection of life, we suddenly gain insight into that wholeness rather than just a small aspect of our separate lives.

For example, every time you pull slightly on a cat's tail, it makes a sound. But if you didn't know that the cat's tail and mouth are connected, you would think these are two separate events, and you might wonder why they happen in such close proximity to each other. This is because we experience so many events in our world as separate. But, while they might be in time and space, they are connected in the non-physical dimension of consciousness, of Spirit. We discover this truth as we witness natural disasters happening all over the world as a result of our collective habits. Before, we didn't think our actions impacted the planet as we saw ourselves and nature as separate. But we are slowly realizing that we are interconnected and, therefore, interdependent.

The shifts suggested in this book are all designed to invite you into the expansive, spiritual-material wholeness of life, where you have access to a greater field of your consciousness and that of the world around you. From this wider vantage point, you can experience and understand firsthand the interconnectedness of all things. And just like the roots of trees or the fungal mycelium underneath our feet, you gain access to valuable information from what you may have originally perceived as separate but now know is intricately connected to you.

Are you familiar with the Hoberman Ball? It is a toy that can collapse and expand. In its expanded form, you can see that all its parts are connected and form a whole circle. If you envision yourself as a point on this ball, you can imagine you are integral to what makes up its entirety. You are in closer proximity to certain parts of the ball, but you are still connected to the entire ball. And just like we are discovering that trees communicate through their root system, so do you gain useful information about the wholeness of your life when you shift into a more expansive state of mind and being.

All this is to explain that when you tap into the interconnected wholeness of life, which the shifts in this book are designed to do, you can communicate with the non-physical dimensions of life because you are part of them. And when you are less connected and more in touch with your separateness, you have less access to the wisdom of the whole, which is when you may feel overwhelmed, lonely, forsaken, and hopeless. And that's why practicing the Principle of Physical and Non-Physical Synergy is crucial for your healing, growth, and transformation.

Now, as everything is conscious and has intelligence, from single atoms and molecules to complex ecological and human systems, we can communicate with seemingly inanimate objects in our surroundings. Whether crafted from nature or invented by human creativity, all objects have life for us to interact with. I developed this capability through my studies with David Spangler, who developed Incarnational Spirituality. Through my ongoing studies with him, I have discovered that every aspect of our world is a field of conscious awareness and has particular properties, even personality. Some objects may feel less alive to us than the natural world, but still, they offer us their conscious awareness, which we can talk to and receive messages from, even though we have been taught they are inanimate.

Many of us talk with different objects in our surroundings without even thinking. You may speak with your deceased aunt when you look at her photo on your bookshelf. You may gain strength and even guidance from your deceased aunt just by communicating with an object that reminds you of her. You may have a favorite stone you put on the desk and connect with before you begin a work session. You might feel that it centers you and brings focus to your work. I would suggest that your favorite stone offers you qualities it possesses, enhancing your workspace with, for example, focus and ease. The beauty of the stone or its unique shape offers you a doorway into its non-physical properties. Your appreciation of this stone enhances its force and influence on your work environment. In this way, physical and non-physical synergy occurs.

For some people, talking to things is second nature; for others, this may be something new to explore and experiment with. I want you to realize that everything in your world is alive and made of consciousness. Everything created by humans holds within it the intention and qualities with which it was created. The more you become aware of the non-physical dimension of your physical world, the more you can live with intention and surround yourself with things that nourish you and will enhance your life. Then, when you interact with your environment, whether it is the natural environment or the human-created physical objects that surround you, you will feel more connected to everything. The more you practice being in relationship with your physical world and perceive the hidden non-physical properties contained within it, the more you can feel that you are participating and co-creating with a living and relational world.

This single Principle of Physical and Non-Physical Synergy can shift your relationship to your home environment, your workspace, the clothes you wear, your car, your exercise equipment, and your relationship to money. All it takes is for you to start talking to everything around you as if it were alive and then listen and stay open to what comes back to you. As you build your relationship with your surroundings, you will discover how much wisdom, insight, and appreciation is hidden around you, ready to support your daily living. You will stop feeling alone and begin to feel that you are part of a living community.

As a result, you'll be able to design an area in your house where you feel, for example, extra creative or productive because you made it come alive with certain elements that inspire you. You will pick your clothes for the day after a conversation with yourself and your wardrobe about the outfit that most fits your mood and intention. And money will no longer just be metal coins and paper, but rather a living entity of great intelligence that can guide you toward wealth. I invite you to explore this expansive perspective of your world, a perspective that enhances spiritual-material wholeness and offers you wisdom at your fingertips.

*Which element of your current situation would you like to communicate with to gain greater clarity and direction?*

# Reflection Prompt

Now that you know that your life's purpose is to experience itself as fully as possible, you can choose how you would like to practice that today. You can choose any part of your life, any activity you need to engage with, or any emotion or quality you want to express more fully. You can also choose to perceive the world around you more fully and decide what you want to focus on appreciating today. You know now that the meaning of life comes with staying aware of the divine essence of everything around you and staying connected to your inner divinity.

Be mindful of the Principle of Spiritual-Material Wholeness and practice staying connected to your divine essence when dealing with a particular situation in your life. Can you perceive the preciousness of each aspect of the situation, the beauty it holds, and the desire to come into greater wholeness? While practicing the Expansive Principle, try understanding the situation from a different perspective or from the viewpoint of another person who may be concerned. While training yourself to see through your particular physical circumstances and opening up to the spiritual dimension of your situation, ask yourself, *What is the silver lining in the situation or the spiritual lesson that is presenting itself to me?*

And finally, experiment with the Principle of Physical and Non-Physical Synergy. Ask yourself, *What parts of or players in this situation can I start communicating with?* Have a dialogue with any aspect of your situation, asking that part to enlighten you as to the underlying issues and needs. You will be amazed at the information and profound insight you will receive. Utilizing these principles will enable you to increase your probability of healing relationships, succeeding in your endeavors, and experiencing the holiness of your life and the world. Move forward with openness, love, and care for yourself and all involved.

# Part V: Shifting Your Perception of Yourself

*"We don't think our way into a new kind of living;
we live our way into a new kind of thinking."*

—Parker Palmer

# Who Are You?

When you think of the shift calling you, are you aware of how you perceive yourself due to your current circumstances? What do you tell yourself constantly about yourself? Do you use encouraging words and appreciate yourself, or do you put yourself down constantly for being where you are in the first place? In what ways is your identity tied up to what you are dealing with? And how is your perception of yourself keeping you stuck where you are?

These are all important questions to ask yourself because you will have to shift your perception of yourself to significantly change your life situation. Otherwise, you will sabotage any external action you take as it will not match your inner perception of yourself. You see, you have to come along for the transformation. You can't just work on some external change and stay stuck in your diminished self-perception. And even if you feel that your life is great and you just want it to get better, you still have to change your self-image to make that leap. So, whether you put yourself down constantly or believe in yourself, you will have to shift your self-image to make the shift calling you.

There are probably two parts to your perception of yourself: what you like about yourself, which has gotten you this far, and what you wish could be different and stops you from believing in yourself and going further. So, start by asking yourself what you love about who you are. Take time to appreciate yourself and how far you've come. Then, acknowledge what you desire to shift about your self-perception. If you listen quietly, you will receive an answer from the shift calling you, your ally, who knows what transformation you need. It may feel confusing to have both a positive and a negative perception of yourself. Don't see these as conflicting messages but rather a measure of how far you've come and what shifts you must go through in this next phase.

We all have different identities that can serve or stifle us. They can empower us or make us withdraw. Some identities are worthwhile until we outgrow them. Therefore, how we perceive ourselves can and sometimes must shift. As we examine our identities, we must acknowledge the labels that define us and become the framework in which we experience our place in every situation and relationship. What if we could shift our identity and experience a familiar situation from a new vantage point? How would it affect our conclusions, our interactions, our decisions, and, consequently, the results?

In my twenties, I would identify as anorexic while introducing myself at each Food Addicts Anonymous meeting. This label served me for a time, empowering me to acknowledge I was starving my emotions and affiliate with others going through similar struggles. However, after a few years of engaging in deep inner work, that label began to stifle my identity. I had moved on to deal with other issues and was not using food anymore to manage my emotional state. So, I found that it was no longer useful in my development.

There is a time and a place to shed identities that do not serve us. Saying, "I'm broke," "broken," or "battered" are temporary labels. If we attach our identities to them, we risk distorting our worldviews—even excluding ourselves from possibilities.

The point is not to erase these labels but to build identities that expand with time. The truth is that some identities we hold onto cause division, make our world smaller, and limit our potential. I don't want that for you. Instead, I invite you to take on a shift in your identity, one that empowers, embraces, receives, and offers the world without judgment, predisposition, or callousness.

In the following pages, I want to offer you potential shifts in your perception of yourself that reflect a deeper sense of who you are and can become at the core—a new lens to perceive yourself and deal with your circumstances. These shifts can offer you a much bigger vision of who you truly are and allow you to grasp how shifting your perceptions can empower you to break through the mold in which you live.

The perceptions I'm about to offer you are radically life-affirming. They will remind you who you are at your essence and allow you to expand your perception of yourself. As you read, ask yourself, *How can I shift from how I perceive myself in relation to the particular issue I'm dealing with to seeing myself in this new, expansive, and life-affirming manner? What do I need to do to take the next step toward seeing myself in such a life-affirming and loving way?* Whatever your circumstances, whatever twists and turns are ahead, you will find this shift in your self-perception a liberating journey of empowerment.

**Which of your identities do you like and want to keep, and which perception of yourself would you like to shift?**

# You Are Consciousness

My spouse offered me the gift of a new perception of myself one day when he recounted a particularly potent meditation session he had experienced. He was eager to share, saying, "Suddenly, I found myself out in space and experienced myself as this beautiful and peaceful point of consciousness in the universe. It was a sacred moment of presence and acknowledgment of my existence."

As I listened, I immediately felt a huge expansion of my being. I was able to experience myself as a being of pure awareness. It felt like a superpower of knowledge and wisdom. In this state, I didn't feel bound by the familiar human identities I had been given or worked hard to create. Instead, I felt free and yet very present. It felt like the purest form of being myself.

It wasn't a dissociative experience of being shapeless and floating aimlessly in space. Instead, it felt like the origin of who I truly am. I was still myself, but I had accessed the essence of myself. It felt liberating and empowering.

This realization blew me away. I was instantly able to shift my self-perception. Instead of seeing myself through the habitual identities I had carried throughout my life—being a woman, an Israeli, or even a human being—I felt free as a field of conscious intelligence within infinite creative potential. This simple truth afforded me a sense of great power. It grabbed me and wouldn't let go.

What touched me the most was that I experienced my own presence in the world. It made me realize, very clearly, that I exist in the cosmos regardless of how small I am in the face of the sun and the planets and even in the face of humanity. While I can't explain the origin of how I came into being, I am here with everyone and everything else that exists in the Cosmos, and if I have a place in this world, then I am worthy to exist.

In the larger scheme of creation, my purpose and capabilities differ from a star in the sky or a whale in the ocean. But we each have a place in this world and something meaningful to contribute to the wholeness of creation. And, as a being of conscious awareness, I can share my unique gifts and talents with my world and whomever I influence and touch in my daily interactions.

We often hear about the power of the subconscious mind, where hidden forces drive our beliefs and actions. But we overlook the power of being conscious. We are alive with awareness. Shifting our identity toward being conscious automatically awakens our senses, offering us an amplified human experience so that we can observe the ride and be more intentional in directing and enjoying it. To quote James Taylor's song "Secret O' Life," "Nobody knows how we got to the top of the hill. But since we're on our way down, we might as well enjoy the ride."

After this profound realization, which felt simultaneously expansive and focused, I began expanding my awareness as a point of consciousness in the universe. I accepted my sacred place in my world, this planet, and all creation. I would imagine myself as a seemingly small point of consciousness within a vast, dark space. I could see my place amid the limitless enormity, offering a worthy presence to honor and respect.

It doesn't matter if my influence seemed microscopic compared to the sun or the planets. I can use my awareness to impact *my* world and increase the reach of *my* influence because I can reflect, create, generate, and expand *my* potential.

Borrowing from my spouse's revelation, I invite you to take a meditative moment now. Can you imagine yourself as a point of consciousness unrelated to any particular earthly identity? It may take practice to see yourself for a moment letting go of all the categories in which others have put you or in which you have had to fit because of how others perceive you. Try to suspend any identity for which you have fought hard to be acknowledged by others. You can come back and embrace all your identities in a moment, but just for a short while, see how it feels to let go of your life story and perceive your essence.

That is an expansive perspective on your life and being as a whole. All the other perceptions of yourself still exist, and you can sense into each one of them and see how it feels in relation to being a point of consciousness in the universe. Begin by taking a moment to experience yourself as a being of conscious awareness, someone with a place in the world and gifts to share with those with whom you interact. To quote Mary Oliver's famous poem "Wild Geese," "Whoever you are, no matter how lonely, the world offers itself to your imagination, calls to you like the wild geese, harsh and exciting, over and over, announcing your place in the family of things."

*When it comes to the shift calling you, how does knowing you exist as a point of consciousness in our world influence your sense of worthiness?*

# You Are a Portal

When we feel stuck, all too often, our unspoken identity is that of a container. We contain potential that is sealed away. Or we subconsciously believe our power is contained by forces, circumstances, and people in our lives. Let me suggest another shift that can reveal your true beauty. It's the shift of envisioning yourself as a portal between the spiritual and material realms. Let's just grasp the concept of being a portal. We are much more than skin and bones.

As humans, we have the capacity to travel between the non-physical and the physical, between imagining and manifesting, visioning and materializing, dreaming and creating. We can bring into material existence anything we can imagine. Now, material creation will, of course, be constrained by circumstances and conditioning, like physical laws, the technology available at the time, and whatever beliefs we hold about what's possible or not possible to create. But being constrained does not mean it's impossible. On the contrary, many times, constriction makes us even more creative.

This incredible ability makes us a portal through which the yet unrealized possibilities of creation can manifest in our earthly existence. That makes us creators of realized opportunity. Becoming a portal of hope is a mighty superpower. But, we might take this for granted. Rather than dismissing this by thinking, *"That's just what humans do,"* embrace this expansive identity. You may have never considered yourself a potent portal for the non-physical to manifest through you in the physical world and for spiritual wisdom to express itself in your daily, seemingly mundane material living. But let me assure you: You are a portal between the spiritual and material realms, and you can experience your own unique desires, imagination, values, life purpose, and capabilities. This shift in your perception of yourself offers a playground for creative collaboration between non-physical potentials and your unique, soulful expression.

Being a portal holds great power. So, set free the hopes, dreams, and desires contained within you. Then, allow possibilities into your life. You'll be amazed at how this simple shift can bring dreams into reality. You can begin by looking back at the last year of your life. What has happened in this previous year that didn't exist before? Is there a particular professional project you were part of forming and running that didn't exist a few months ago? What role did you have in imagining and designing the phases of this project? I know we take this for granted because it is just what we do all the time, but it's miraculous. You begin with a desire, a need, or a requirement, and then you use your imagination, knowledge, and capabilities to bring it into being. You use the help of other professionals, or you collaborate with others to give your project form. Whatever you've created, you have birthed it into being.

Stop and think about that for just a moment. Something that didn't exist before now exists because you breathed life into it. We have created an entire civilization by starting with a desire or a need, imagining how we might bring it form, and then using our capabilities to realize it.

Take a moment to experience yourself as a portal between the non-physical and the physical and a creator who can make flesh your desires and your imagination. You can then begin to feel how capable and powerful you are and how magical your life can be. But you have to expand your view of yourself and begin to perceive yourself as a miracle of creation. Even if you only catch fleeting moments of this plane of existence, a glimpse into your true nature, it is a wonder-filled start. Keep practicing, expanding, and shifting your perception of yourself as a portal between the spiritual and material realms.

Then ask yourself, *How can I become a portal for spiritual wisdom to express itself in my life and guide me as I shift forward?*

**When it comes to the particular shift you desire, how does realizing you are a magical portal between the spiritual and material worlds change your innate sense of power?**

# You Are a Conduit

You can identify with different activities you perform in the world, such as your profession, hobbies, and other occupations you engage with. Or you can identify with different roles you play, like being a mom or someone's sister. You can be identified by your race, ethnicity, gender, and so on. All these are mostly fixed identities you have been given or have grown into. They don't offer much fluidity and flexibility, at least not in our mainstream culture. Even if you feel that you have evolved, others may put a label on you that can feel very stifling, or you may trap yourself in an identity without noticing that you are limiting yourself.

But what if you could perceive yourself as a conduit of spiritual qualities that you bring forth into everything you do and all your interactions? You may ask, *what does that even mean, a conduit of qualities that would enhance the value of each moment?* Let me explain what I mean and why I suggest this can offer you greater flexibility than some of your more traditional perceptions of yourself. It will result in a much greater sense of agency and is therefore essential to shift-making and effecting real change.

A quality is a state of mind, an attitude we perceive or express. Qualities include different attributes in our language, such as joy, grandeur, power, peace, contentment, enthusiasm, acceptance, ease, focus, care, firmness, curiosity, and thousands more. Qualities don't just embellish a sentence you say; they enhance an experience and amplify a situation. For example, the following qualities alter the experience of each statement: The ocean was tranquil. Or, the ocean was rough. My trip back home was enjoyable, or it was exhausting. My breakup was devastating, or it was necessary. These descriptions add layers of emotion to what you are experiencing. They can bring each moment to life with depth, intensity, and a better understanding of your experience.

You can decide to use qualities intentionally by becoming a conduit of different qualities for different occasions. For example, when going home to visit family, you could imagine yourself as a conduit of the quality of authenticity or tranquility. How might that alter your next holiday visit back home? If you practice being a conduit for either of these qualities, maybe you'll end up having a heart-to-heart talk with a family member that will bring you closer, or you might be able to bring calming resolution to a family argument.

For a team meeting, you could decide to be a conduit of the quality of creativity. How would that influence the effectiveness of the weekly Monday morning meeting and the enjoyment of everyone present? It might elevate everyone's experience from the habitual rote meeting of checking off items from a to-do list to an inspiring meeting of minds and finding more creative ways to collaborate. The possibilities are endless when you pair a quality with a situation you are facing, a challenge you are dealing with, or a setting you want to intentionally and positively influence. You become a conduit for that quality and imbue the situation with that quality.

You can even blend qualities and layer them. You can become a conduit of peaceful power when standing up to injustice, a conduit of focus, patience, and ease when working on something that takes time and requires attention to detail, and a conduit of caring and spaciousness when supporting a friend or family member trying to find their way in life. By becoming a conduit for these qualities, you become an influencer in the situation. You sprinkle the energetic essence of qualities that help move things forward in a life-affirming and favorable manner. You elevate the entire situation, linking the materially mundane and the spiritually inspiring. From my experience, it can feel very empowering to take on these fluid identities, as if they have a life of their own. And they do!

As a conduit of qualities, your focus is less on your role as it is defined culturally or professionally and more on how you express yourself at any given moment. Instead of remaining a fixed identity that was defined way back and didn't change, you can become a fluid conduit of qualities that have the power to amplify any situation and bring about more favorable interactions and solutions. You can adjust to any situation and become a conduit for what you feel is relevant to the specific setting.

If I asked a group of people what peacefulness meant to them, they would have many overlapping responses, some unique to their experience. The same is with any other quality. We know what it means when we say that a tree in the park evokes grandeur or that a person we met for the first time oozes confidence. These are not just words in the English language; they are living words with energetic presence that bring our daily experiences and special moments to life. Because of that, they can help you shift with greater ease as they offer release from stuck identities that keep you trapped in how you look and feel, what you believe you are able to do in your life, and what changes you can bring about.

Know that you may have easier access to certain emotions or qualities than others. These are your unique gifts to share with your world. We inherit some from our parents and others from our life experiences. We are also born with easy access to certain qualities, while others seem harder to access. You may have learned the quality of steadfastness and have easy access to continue moving forward in the face of adversity. But, you may have never learned how to be kind to yourself and so have a more challenging time accessing the quality of kindness.

You can decide, for example, to practice getting better at being a conduit of joy if that is something that you find challenging to bring into your day. Life circumstances and past experiences may not have allowed you to practice much joy. But you really want to bring more joy into your life. Play with shifting your identity as a conduit of qualities and observe what happens.

The most important thing is to remember that life is ever-changing from moment to moment, so you don't want to stay stuck with a particular quality just because, in certain circles, they may value it more than other qualities. For example, in spiritual circles, peacefulness and compassion seem to be valued above the huge range of qualities available to us. While they are useful in many situations, I have found that adhering to the same qualities can dull your experience and make you more judgmental of others if you become rigid about always attaching to them. Instead, feel the freedom of flowing from one quality to another based on what the situation calls for. For example, experiment with being a conduit of delight and enthusiasm when those qualities are most needed in a particular situation.

Everything is possible. You can even go meta and decide to be a conduit of love to all your existing identities, those you love, and those you would prefer to go away. You may discover a hidden gift in these identities, an underlying and neglected need you would like to address, or a value you hold dear. This process in itself could be life-changing. So, pick the qualities with which you would like to imbue your day or a particular situation and experience how becoming a conduit for these particular qualities will move you forward on your path.

*When it comes to the shifts you want to make, how does knowing that you can impact your interactions and circumstances help you become a more potent influencer?*

# You Are Creative Intelligence

We get so caught up in our human world that we forget we play a vital role in this vast universe and magnificent planet. Understandably, we become narrow-sighted because of endless daily demands to the point that we forget to stop and marvel at a small honey bee flying from flower to flower and pollinating our entire planet. We forget to recognize the ingenious design of a spider web catching morning dew for the spider to drink; humans as the creative force on our planet, developing an entire civilization from what grows above and below the soil. Putting it this way, it's pretty incredible, wouldn't you say?

While we can lose sight of the natural wonders around us, consumed with the daily pressures and deadlines, I'd like to offer you a shift in your perception of yourself that will help you stay aligned with your power and place in your life: You are creative intelligence.

How do I know this? Because you are also a creative expression of creation. And so is everything within you, from the cells in your body to the complexity of being a spiritual, emotional, physical, and social being who can reflect, foster meaningful relationships, and, in return, be a creative and generative source in our world. As a complex, highly evolved, innovative form of intelligence, you can imagine and bring virtually anything into form.

Taking it a step further, consider that everything you can perceive with your senses or can experience, even if it does not have a physical form, is a field of creative intelligence. We often perceive our physical world as solid and ideas and emotions as benign and ephemeral thoughts that come and go. But, as I spoke of in Part IV, The Substance of Life, both the non-physical and physical realms of our existence are made up of different defined fields of intelligent energy that vibrate at different frequencies and appear to have different levels of density. Each one has its unique properties, capabilities, and identity. And they all come together into different constellations and creative collaborations, creating life-affirming possibilities of wonder all around us.

A hydrogen atom has its singular identity, properties, and capabilities. It is a unique field of creative intelligence. Likewise, an oxygen atom has a distinctive identity, properties, and capabilities, making it a classifiable field of creative intelligence. And when two molecules of hydrogen come together with a molecule of oxygen, then we have water, the substance that covers 71 percent of the surface of our planet and makes up 60 percent of our bodies. Water is a significant aspect of our life. What creative intelligence in these two little atoms.

Now I know that unless you are a chemistry buff, you might not care much about hydrogen and oxygen molecules and don't see how that might relate to you making a significant shift in your life. Well, think about this. If two small atoms can come together to sustain your body and create the conditions for life on our planet, can you imagine what you, who are infinitely more complex, might be able to do if you decide to use your creative intelligence to express yourself more fully in this world? And what will we be able to do if humanity joins forces, like the hydrogen and oxygen molecules, to create something life-affirming and wondrous?

Take a moment to imagine yourself as a field of creative intelligence. Close your eyes so you can go inward and avoid being distracted by the external world. Envision your entire being—body and soul—as a field of potent intelligence. Every cell in your body is magnificently structured for a particular purpose, functioning in cooperation with all the other cells in your body. Feel yourself as an infinite field of creative intelligence. Become aware of your intricate potential to imagine something and bring it into creation. Affirm yourself for being an incredibly complex human capable of creating out of your pure desire and imagination. That is also a creative collaboration between your non-physical imagination and whatever other aspects of yourself are involved in bringing your thoughts to life.

Once you can sense the life-affirming and powerful wonder that you are, ask yourself, *How does this expanded perception of myself help me shift what I'm dealing with right now?* Take the time to listen to the infinite wisdom waiting to reveal itself to you.

***When it comes to your unique life circumstances, in what ways does knowing you are a sophisticated creative being connect you to your innate power?***

# You Are a Pollinator

When shifting our perception of ourselves, we must move beyond our roles in life. We're more than spouses, parents, children, siblings, co-workers, or friends. While our actions or employment can define our identities, we are more than athletes, writers, doctors, attorneys, or actors in this real-life play. Unfortunately, our identities can also be chained up by our self-defeating beliefs, like being boring, incapable, stuck, unsure, lost, and confused. These roles, actions, and beliefs may have some truth, but let me suggest an identity shift in your perception that serves others as it serves you.

I learned this lesson from the almighty bee. Before assuming that I'm referring to becoming "busy as a bee," I want to remind you that bees have a beautifully powerful duty that serves a greater good—for their species and plant and human life. Their identity is a pollinator.

On a sunny afternoon, I visited a friend who is an avid gardener. She has created a little haven in her backyard with different corners to sit and take a break from the business of life. Her garden is filled with plants, flowers, birds, and bees. That particular day, I decided to enjoy a moment of peaceful meditation in one of the garden's enclaves as nature buzzed around me.

In a meditative state, I opened my eyes to observe the bushes surrounding me. I felt myself melting as the sun's warmth slowly thawed the tension in my body. A breeze offered a mild caress on my face, calling my attention to the present moment. I could feel myself slowing down, allowing the elements to cradle me as I became more immersed in the garden. I was reminded that I, too, am part of the natural world.

Soon, my gaze focused on the nearest bush adorned with gray leaves and small purple flowers. I observed its delicate petals, perfectly designed for a bee to settle into for a few seconds to capture some nectar and pollen before flying off to the next purple attraction. The more attention I gave this bush, the more bees I saw moving from flower to flower, landing on the bottom petal of a flower, hovering for a few seconds, and then backing out and moving to the next flower.

Suddenly, I became even more still as one particular bee made its way closer and closer to me. It came to a flower very near my face. Without flinching, I watched it hover for a while. I could see its eyes. Its wings had such intricate and complex magnificence. I thought to myself, *I am experiencing, in real-time, what normally is reserved for hidden cameras relaying images for televised nature shows.* After the brief encounter, the bee moved on, giving me a minute to digest the unique moment.

In the midst of this expansive instant of bliss, a bee-inspired insight dropped into my mind: *We, humans, are like pollinating bees, and we are each a flower that is being pollinated by other human bees*. I could feel my excitement rising as I contemplated this thought.

Bees play a part in every aspect of the ecosystem. They support the growth of trees, flowers, and other plants, which serve as food and shelter for creatures large and small. Bees contribute to complex, interconnected ecosystems that allow a diverse number of different species to coexist. They also provide us with honey, beeswax, glue, and venom, allowing us to prepare an antidote. We depend on bees for our very existence. Without bees, our ecosystem wouldn't have the pollination it needs to survive.

Like bees, we pollinate others with our thoughts, insights, conclusions, and creative ideas throughout the day, whether with a colleague at work, a friend during lunch, the cashier in the store, or a family member at home. Conversely, we are like flowers, receiving pollination from everyone and everything around us. That same colleague at work, friend at lunch, cashier at the store, or family member share their thoughts, projects, and opinions on the state of the world. It's a constant exchange of pollination that connects us to new ideas, trying new things, or taking action in a new and improved manner. My friend's garden is a microcosm of life, and likewise, we need to accept our role as pollinators that feed a greater good for ourselves, our communities, and our world.

Becoming a pollinator is more than just the exercise of exchanging information. Rather, our perception of ourselves as pollinators brings intent and, consequently, more meaning and purpose. If we perceive ourselves as a flower being pollinated by other bees, we will become more selective and intentional about who we want to allow into the pistil of our being and more attentive when receiving the gifts of pollination offered to us throughout our day. Like bees, we become careful about who and what we offer others while filtering what pollinates us.

Although our intent as pollinators is to give and glean qualities to improve our existence, we may not always know when it's happening. People who have influenced us may be unaware of how influential they have been in our life. Likewise, there are people we have influenced who may or may not remember that we shaped an aspect of their life. It's the beautiful cosmic irony of receiving a gift from a seemingly anonymous source. For example, I once connected with an old friend on Facebook who I had not been in touch with for decades. Through our messages, I discovered my friend had been baking a chocolate cake from a recipe I had, supposedly, given her 30 years earlier. Although I did not remember the recipe or giving it to her, I was touched by how I had contributed to creating many special chocolate cake memories for her without even being part of her life anymore.

My insight about humans being super pollinators was not due to a deductive thought process but rather a piece of wisdom that became available to me while opening myself to the wisdom available from the larger whole of nature. It was an honor to receive such a massive concept from such a seemingly little source—which, in reality, is responsible for 80 percent of all plant pollination on our planet.

I don't want you to think of all this as a metaphor. Instead, I want you to consider it possible to practice seeing yourself as a pollinating bee and a receptive flower. If you do it with a sacred Intention, then you are like the bee, gently pollinating nature, humanity, and our planet. It's a simple shift in our perception of ourselves. Accepting this shift leads to an open-ness and confidence to be of service and be served. It's a beau-tiful shift with massive rewards! Ever since that morning when that little bee greeted me in my friend's garden, I've taken on a shift in perception that I, too, can pollinate the world. By sharing this insight, I hope to pollinate you with this expansive idea that offers endless possibilities.

*How can your perception of yourself as a pollinator improve your relationships?*

# Your Life is An Occasion

The world becomes ripe with opportunities as we shift our perception of ourselves into a more expansive mindset. The way we view life, and the experiences within it, opens the door to creative expression. Our previous perception of ourselves may have provided a safety net, but too often, we get tangled in its web. Moving our identities beyond our roles, affiliations, and what we were born with offers a foundational perspective to experience more from life and the ability to transform with it.

As a point of consciousness, we bring presence. As a portal, we allow the free flow of ideas from the spiritual realm to the material. As creative intelligence, we tap into ingenuity. As a pollinator, we serve while being served. All these shifts in our perception of ourselves lead to a conclusion, which comes from one of my favorite lines from a wonderful movie with a funny title, *Mr. Magorium's Wonder Emporium.* In one of the final scenes, Mr. Magorium is preparing his apprentice, whom he has trained to become the store manager of his magical toy store, for his departure from life. His apprentice urges him to stay, telling him that she is not ready for him to leave. As he moves closer to her, he takes her hands, looks into her eyes, and says:

*"Your life is an occasion. Rise to it."*

Like Mr. Magorium, I encourage you to shift your perception of yourself to one that experiences your unique life as an occasion worthy of rising to. I'm inviting you to this occasion. You just need to RSVP. You aren't meant to shield yourself from life, nor is your life defined exclusively by your past. Instead, every moment, every interaction, and every circumstance offers you an occasion, an opportunity to transform into the person you want to be. When we embrace the occasion, we find fulfillment, empowerment, hope, and love. We find ourselves living our life more fully while serving the greater good.

***What awakens in you when you fully take in that your life is a uniquely precious occasion?***

# Reflection Prompt

I have shared some significant shifts you can try around your perception of yourself. I'm sure you have noticed that I have picked self-perceptions that are less defined by our culture and more universal. These offer you an expanded experience of yourself, with ample room to grow into a larger version of yourself. Just picking one of these identities and working with it for a week or a month can be transforming. So, don't feel the need to practice them all. Instead, you can try each one for a day and see how it feels, and then pick the one that most calls you and practice it for longer. You can return to each of these again and again, finding new meaning and discovering new insights each time.

As you play with these self-perceptions and shift between them, sense how each one feels in your body or what feeling it evokes. You will be surprised by how much information you will discover about the different identities you live by. You will also be able to remember that you are more than one particular identity. You are more than the medical diagnosis you live with, the family situation you were born into, or your economic status. And if you are more than any of those identities, you can develop any identity you desire and begin creating it here and now. Step into a larger, more loving, and enlightened version of yourself and see what opens up in you. Welcome it in, and let it guide you. As the saying goes, *what you are longing for, is also seeking you.*

# Part VI: Shifting Your Perspective of Our World

*"Another world is not only possible, she is on her way;
on a quiet day I can hear her breathing."*

—Suzanna Arundhati Roy

# From Deception to Authenticity

Previous generations have never been so enamored with deception. The beauty industry is built on it. Social media perpetuates it. The news media feeds on it. And we buy into it. The truth is unexpected these days. Deception is so prevalent that finding the truth is like trying to solve a puzzle—except there's one piece missing.

Our self-deception works against the natural laws of the universe, blocking us from expanding into greater levels of awareness. For example, we may tell ourselves that "we're in control" when we're clearly not. Or that we "will never amount to much" when it's clearly possible to accomplish a lot. Perhaps we lie about our appearance when beauty is clearly from within. In all these examples, we are deceiving ourselves. We are either inflating or belittling our power and self-worth. With these blockages, we take on skewed perceptions of reality. Underneath our default mode to deceive, we're expressing fear, which can take on many forms; fear of what others may think or say, fear of being exposed, fear of being blamed, fear of being hurt or of hurting others. And underneath that fear is a profound lack of worthiness. So, we put on rose-colored lenses and defend "our truth," effectively moving ground zero from the natural and honest flow of life.

To transform our world, we have to shift from deception to authenticity.

Here we can learn a great lesson from addicts in recovery, embracing the principles of humility and honesty that define Step One of the famous Twelve Steps. For addicts, hiding the truth becomes second nature. Unable to face their problems, they tell themselves they are "in control" and justify the abuse of drugs and alcohol with every fiber of their being. Resorting to admission would mean they have to be humble enough to recognize they have an addiction that has taken their life way off course and honestly admit the truth to themselves and others.

But when they do, a miracle occurs. The weight of deception is lifted when they become willing to look honestly at themselves and their lives. The rose-colored lenses come off, and they can examine the reality of what led them to addiction in the first place. The truth and being authentic become a refreshing salve for their soul and a safe place to explore.

The fact is, we all may have varying degrees of addiction to deception. In this addiction, we can tell ourselves we're in control and that nobody will learn the truth, but we're only perpetuating more deception. The cost adds up. Without trust, relationships suffer. Without truth, we can't honestly look at our problems. Without humility, we can never grow. Basically, we stop ourselves from becoming our best selves. We become enslaved to deception. As a wise friend once said, "if you fight for your limitations, you get to keep them."

Shifting from deception to authenticity takes more than just flipping a switch. It takes practice, but it's also the result of something deeper coming to the surface. As I've mentioned, deception is baked in fear. But if we can forgive ourselves and others while accepting responsibility for our words and actions, then we can find authenticity.

Too often, we're quick to blame others for making us feel or react in certain ways. But as addicts know, being authentic means taking responsibility "for our side of the ledger" in humility. Rather than blame others, we need to be responsible for ourselves, our thoughts, words, and actions. Rather than assign blame, we can hold compassion for others who act out their self-deceptions, perhaps in unsavory ways. A value I hold dearly is owning my thoughts, actions, and words. Taking this responsibility helps me avoid blaming others while freeing myself by owning my part.

Taking ownership does not mean blaming yourself for one more thing you didn't do right. We don't need more blame. We carry enough self-blame from our past, and when we become honest with ourselves, we can see how it has infected nearly every viewpoint of life. Our perspectives get twisted with the lies. So being honest with ourselves can sound like another way to remind us of that blame and permit a little more self-hatred. But we don't need to short-change ourselves any longer.

Instead, we take ownership of the truth about ourselves, not the lies we've heard from others. We're honest about who we are at our essence and how we are short-changing ourselves with the roles we play, words we choose, and actions we take. This expansive perspective is always greater, more life-affirming, and more loving. It always wants you to be more fully who you are. It's liberating to release a huge amount of stuck energy, resources, and capabilities and begin using them to better your situation, life, and world.

When you are dealing with the shift calling you, you can accept the limitations of the situation, but you can also accept the possibilities this situation offers. If you focus only on what is currently happening in your life, it may seem like you are authentically and truthfully examining the facts. But you are also deceiving yourself by not looking at the possibilities for bettering your situation and the opportunities for healing, growth, and transformation. If you stay focused on the limitations of your situation, you may think that you are being realistic. Still, I want you to entertain a shift in your perspective, where you are deceiving yourself by limiting the range of empowering, creative, life-affirming, and loving solutions.

Avoiding this place of authentic living comes from an underlying, soulful need or unmet desire. I can't be sure what that need or desire is for you, but I know that finding the ability to forgive and taking ownership of yourself with humble honesty can shift you from deception to authenticity. If you don't do that, you'll continue living in a facade with surface-level relationships and remain stuck in fear. However, if you tap into your authentic self, the world opens up as your fears get laid to rest. It is then that you can develop a loving relationship with yourself, others, and the world.

As the saying goes, "The truth will set you free." You are not alone in the universe and don't have to rely on yourself to survive. You don't have to compete for riches, beauty, or power. Instead, you can align with the truth. You don't have to hold fast to prevalent, false, and deceptive beliefs that keep you separate, small, and fearful. When you shift your perspective, you can begin to see that you live in an abundant, kind, and generous world striving toward connection, wholeness, beauty, creative expression, profound meaning, and purpose. This is one shift you should no longer avoid.

So, ask yourself, *In what ways do I deceive myself?* Do I inflate my power, or do I diminish and minimize my agency, capabilities, and wisdom? How can I be more authentic, and how can I love myself more when I am authentic? Asking these questions without self-judgment will allow you to release what doesn't serve you anymore so that you can start embracing your authentic and precious self and, in turn, transition from deception to authenticity in all areas of your life.

***What is a simple, underlying, truthful statement about your unique situation that can empower you and set you free?***

# From Isolation to Connection

When we feel stressed and anxious, we often go into survival mode, which makes us feel even more isolated, just when we most need support and connection. It's oddly ironic, but that is what we often do. Here's the thing. We wouldn't feel so stressed and isolated if we looked for support and connection when we needed it the most. The fact is that stress and isolation breed more stress and isolation, and likewise, support and connection breed more support and connection. So, why do we often retreat into isolation when we most need connection?

I believe it comes from thinking that we are separate instead of part of the living wholeness of life. You may ask, how does that relate to my immediate growing anxiety? Well, it has to do with a deeply ingrained human thought that has trickled down to our daily thinking without us even noticing. But it affects every aspect of our personal life, as well as our collective existence. Let me explain.

First, to make a shift in our perspective, we need to understand how we came to think of ourselves as separate and isolated. We come into this world as separate beings and leave this world each in our own time. Life on planet Earth is expressed through individuation, whether human, animal, plant, or mineral. Each species expresses its unique properties, and each human expresses their singularity. And our human brain is an expert in classifying and codifying everything we perceive as our way to orient ourselves and make meaning of our world. So, it is natural that we experience ourselves as separate from the rest of the world around us. In addition, we have been taught for centuries that we are separate and need to fend for ourselves. It is ingrained in our neurological wiring.

Imagine our ancestors looking out into the vast skies. It must have felt overwhelming and scary to perceive themselves as separate and alone, small and helpless, in the face of this vast universe. Do you feel this way when you look up into the night skies? Now, add to that our innate instinct for self-preservation—this survival instinct innate to all species. Suddenly, we need to ensure that we are the strongest and can outsmart everyone else because if we don't, we might not survive. We may need to kill to persist and, suddenly, the means justify the end.

You can see how over the centuries, this belief of separation combined with a strong survival instinct has created social structures of domination to endure. With this thinking, we need access to natural and human resources and ensure we are always at the top to persist over others. And we need to be rich to dominate all these resources. Over time, this thinking that we are separate has created hierarchies. This thinking has brought about horrors such as wars, slavery, torture, rape, abuse of power, pillaging, and destruction of our natural environment, all because we keep believing that we are separate and have to fend for ourselves to survive.

This human belief is handed down from one generation to another. It is held in our culture at large, for example, by nations who fight for their survival, believing they have no other choice, or by tyrants who believe they must conquer neighboring countries to remain the strongest and have access to natural resources. You can see how a seemingly innocent thought can shape the history of humanity and our planet over the ages and cause great suffering and destruction.

This thought form is upheld by us individually, as part of our collective. We each believe that we are alone in this world. And when we feel stressed, we contract instead of expand. We go into fight or flight and isolate ourselves to survive because we believe that no one can help us or would ever want to help us. We have been taught that we are separate and, therefore, alone, so when our self-preservation kicks in, we instinctively contract instead of expand.

But here's the price we pay for holding on to a consciousness of separation. It is based on fear. It is a lonely existence of a constant existential crisis. The meaning of life remains at the level of self-preservation. The only relief is momentary. If we are more the bullish type, then we experience a momentary relief when we have conquered something or someone. And, if we feel more like a victim in life, then we feel a momentary relief when we have escaped the physical or emotional claws of someone. But then we just go back to our survival mode to persevere. After a while, it becomes a habitual pattern that we enact without thinking whether we are truly in danger and must continue fighting alone for survival. Whether we feel we are the bully or a victim of circumstances, it is a mindset of survival of the fittest, destruction of humanity, and conquering nature. It is a harsh existence, and it explains why we would contract and isolate ourselves when we feel stress or trauma.

What if we shifted from this destructive thought form? What if we could shift from isolation to connection? How would that affect our personal situation as well as our global situation—humanity and our planet?

Imagine we begin thinking a different thought, one where we are all connected. What if we adopt the belief that we are interdependent, where we know that when we take care of each other, everyone benefits, and we all thrive? Combining this thinking with our innate survival instinct can produce very different results. It is a life-affirming combination because it implies that we depend on each other for our survival and have to collaborate to persevere. It means we must help each other thrive for everyone to benefit and enjoy a full life.

It is a life-affirming way of thinking because it invites us to feel that we are part of a whole and that we need each other and every species on this planet to persevere and thrive. It brings about a mindset of collaboration with nature and other humans. It has the potential to lead toward creative, empowering, life-affirming solutions that allow everyone involved to thrive and benefit. It implies that each of us, human, animal, plant, and mineral, has a unique value to bring to the whole. It is, therefore, a consciousness of love and caring for each other. It is also a consciousness of safety because we don't assume that someone is out to get us, hurt us, or even kill us for their survival. On the contrary, we stand up for each other. We each have a unique gift to offer the whole, and our well-being is related to the well-being of others.

In this scenario, everything is considered sacred, bringing joy, meaning, and a sense of adventure to discover each other's gifts and contributions to the world. Life seems full of meaning as we see connections between our life and events around us. Everything seems magical as we discover new creative, life-affirming connections that we did not anticipate. We see ourselves as pollinators, and we are open to being pollinated by others. We are more attuned to the interconnection and interdependence of life and are open to new connections. Life is joyous, magical, and full of meaning and purpose.

This is not some imaginary utopian fantasy. It is a reality that happens each time we think and act from a place of connection instead of isolation. And the good news is that today, we have the knowledge and understanding that we need the diversity of humans, animals, plants, and minerals on this planet. We know that we need each other to thrive. We increasingly realize that when one species is destroyed or extinct, it has a domino effect on an entire ecosystem and eventually affects us all. It is becoming clear to us through the effects of climate change in different areas on the planet and our communities who suffer the consequences. And it has become clear through the global experience of the COVID pandemic, which is the first time that humanity has shared a common event at the same time as a species. A painful experience but a lesson that we are interconnected and interdependent. From the perspective of the evolution of human consciousness, this is a huge step toward changing our neurological pathways from separate and isolated to being part of a whole.

These are big evolutionary processes that take time, but they are present in our daily lives, and we have the power to change our thinking in order to hasten this evolution of consciousness. We are the ones who bring this evolution about by shifting our thinking from separation to wholeness, from isolation to connection. So, the next time you feel stressed, know that you hold the balance of the world in your hands. I am not saying this to put any pressure on you. Rather, I say this to remind you that you have the agency and the capability to shift the consciousness of humanity and our planet if you choose to connect instead of isolate the next time you feel stressed. And you have the power to reach out to someone and let them know that you are there for them the next time they feel stressed because you know that helping someone else helps you.

Here is the choice that lies before you. Which will you choose?

When you perceive yourselves as separate, your survival becomes your primary focus, and when you are stressed, isolation seems the only way forward. But if you perceive yourself as a precious part of a loving whole, then your thriving becomes essential to everyone, and likewise, someone else's well-being becomes your well-being and the thriving of all of us. It is a conscious practice of shifting your perspective from isolation to connection, reaching out when you need help, and showing up for others in need, whether they are your close family and friends or someone you don't yet know. Shifting your perspective on your life and our world from isolation to connection will not completely alleviate stress from your life but will allow you to deal with stress in more effective and life-affirming ways and, therefore, get you out of stress with greater ease and more significant results.

*When it comes to the specific shift calling you, what is one thing you can do to shift from being less isolated to feeling more connected to yourself and others?*

# From Senseless to Sacred Gateway

It is a common teaching in spiritual circles that our senses only serve the purpose of physical function in the material world. Even worse, they deceive us and deviate us from the truth within, where we can find our true liberation from our physical existence. But what if we shift our perspective and discover that our senses can nourish our soul and are an important conductor between the physical and non-physical realms? What if we start experiencing our senses as a channel to remain connected with the inner spiritual realms? Well, then, our daily material existence could shift from being purely transactional and meaningless to being filled with joy and fulfillment, meaning and purpose.

I want to share with you how I realized that our senses are masterfully-designed instruments to help us experience the divine essence of our material existence and connect us to the inner, spiritual realms from which all physical things come into existence. My wish is that this account awakens you to the preciousness of your senses and their role in finding deep meaning and purpose.

I was working in my therapy on healing specific child-hood traumas that seemed to still control my life five decades later. On this specific occasion, I recalled a memory from my infancy in the baby nursery during the days following my birth in a hospital. As I was invited to remember the incident through a guided meditation, I saw myself lying in the baby nursery with many other babies around me. My mom was not with me as it was not common, in those days, for babies to stay with their mothers after birth in a hospital, something that horrified me when I heard it as an adult. In addition, my mother had caught an infection after my birth and had a high fever. So, she was kept under surveillance for two extra weeks. During her recovery, I spent most of my time in the baby nursery and was rolled into my mother's room during feeding hours.

When asked to recall how it felt to lie in that baby nursery, I remembered feeling like a very rigid baby, not moving, not complaining, not crying, just wrapped up very tightly in some cloth. I found it so curious that I was so stiff. It made me sad that I was not being held and cared for. But the most shocking realization from this memory was that it was accompanied by an assumption I made that I shouldn't ask for my needs because they won't be met. This was shocking and a very familiar assumption I had held all my life. I even starved my emotions in my early twenties to not have to deal with any feeling or need that I might have.

You can imagine that this was a very painful memory. Still, it also offered the promise of some relief, as the original experience that had proceeded so many other painful experiences throughout my life, where I had denied my needs and paid heavy consequences. I realized that this early assumption had informed all my relationships and many choices I had made, both personally and professionally. I had adopted the mantra that *I shouldn't ask for my needs because they will not be met.* And underneath this assumption was a deeply ingrained belief that kept telling me *I am not worthy of being cared for like a baby should, to be fed, nurtured, nourished, and loved.*

With this heart-wrenching belief having formulated much of my experiences in life, I was invited in this particular therapy session to imagine a resource state. I could pick an image of something or someone that would be a resource for me, nourishing that baby trapped in my memory with this self-harming belief. I could use this image as a resource when the belief that I'm not worthy was triggered and showed up in a situation. With time, I would learn to use this resource state more often and be able to shift more quickly from the old belief to a resourceful one.

The image I chose as my resource state was King T'Challa's tribe of women from the movie *Black Panther*. It is one of my favorite movies, and these women just came to me as soon as I was told to pick someone who could counter my initial experience in infancy. The women in this movie are warrior fighters who keep together and protect each other. They seem to be fully aligned within themselves, grounded, open-hearted, with brilliant minds. I remembered their fierceness, like the lioness fierceness I had experienced as a mom with my two sons, and what I had wanted for myself as a newborn baby.

In my therapy session, I imagined this tribe of women walking into the baby nursery while the nurses told them they could not enter. They just picked me up and took me with them to their home. I saw myself being held by one of them in this beautiful kitchen with a big glass window that looked out onto a secluded wooded forest. I was securely and gently nested in the arms of one of these women. Another woman cooked a meal for everyone. The woman cuddled and sang to me, which defrosted the childhood memory of that frozen baby.

As I imagined myself as this baby being loved and nourished, I realized that the gentle singing from this woman was a bridge between my non-physical essence, from where I had emerged before I was born, and my physical body, which absorbed this love. This bridge connected the Divine Love in the spiritual, non-physical realm with the love in our earthy, physical existence. Love was the language that bridged the two realms through my auditory senses. It was a precious moment that was treated with sacredness. I had been born just a few days before, and I was treated with sacredness as a being who had entered the material world and needed to keep a vital connection with my Source.

During this guided exercise, I had the profound realization that I had come from the nonphysical, as we all do before birth. In the nonphysical, I knew my essence. I knew love, sacredness, and the wholeness of life. And my senses in the physical plane bridged a lifeline to all I knew before I was born. Not only would my senses allow me to experience the material plane in my lifetime, but they would also serve as fine-tuned instruments, allowing me to experience the material plane as a sacred expression of the spiritual, non-physical plane.

                                    Shift Calling

From this new shift in perspective, my senses would bridge my spiritual and material existence. Now that is a true shift in perspective from our senses being a mere physical function of survival or even a distraction from the true spiritual treasures of the inner worlds.

I have come to know our senses in an intentional way, with a heightened awareness and enhanced presence, connecting us to the non-physical, spiritual side in us, to our soul, to where we come from, to our essence. We should use our senses to connect to the sacredness of life around us and within us instead of minimizing them as mere functionality. This is so important to the process of shifting because it can offer our daily life a vibrancy and an aliveness that we find hard to experience when we are unaware of this enchanted gateway. And as our senses make our material world come alive, our existence takes on new meaning, and our unique life experiences can become a divine expression of love, beauty, joy, meaning, and purpose.

*How can you use your senses as a sacred gateway to soothe the places you hurt and experience and express more love in your life?*

# From Illusion to Magical

Many spiritual teachers consider our physical, material world a mere illusion. This belief originates in a fundamental teaching in Buddhism and Hindu philosophy called the veil of *Maya*, a word in Sanskrit meaning illusion, pretense, or deceit. The New Age movement in the west has adopted this idea, preaching that our physical world is not real. Our corporal existence, they claim, serves only for basic transactional necessities of existence, bodily functions, and material enjoyment. However, I believe a shift in perspective is in order. A true spiritual quest consists of seeing through this illusion and finding the magical kingdom in what our senses perceive, and our heart can take in.

I do not accept that the material world is an illusion. It doesn't align with the wondrous natural world surrounding us and the ingenuity of human creation over the centuries. Why should the material world be treated as here today, gone tomorrow, and on to the landfill? Aren't inner peace, joy, and contentment equally elusive and transient? And what if we could perceive our material world as an expression of the inner spiritual realms? Having spent a decade living in Paris, France, and traveling throughout Europe and the world, I've come to respect all creation as exalting and craftsmanship as a devotional and dedicated expression of a Divine Source.

For example, wouldn't you agree that English gardens have magnificent beauty and aromas, and their gardeners have engaged with nature to nurture its growth? This is no illusion. I've also experienced the wonders of French craftsmanship, whether in fashion, architecture, or cooking. These expressions have resulted from a methodical pursuit of perfection crafted with love through creative inspiration. When humans produce ingenuity with precision, the results are magical.

Why deny our physical existence, writing it off as an aberration? Why should human creation be trivialized as devoid of the magic and wonder of our world? Something else is going on here that is far more creative, life-affirming, and a glorious hymn to creation. And you and I are an integral part of it, generative sources creating magic in our world.

Perhaps we need to accept the alternative translation for the word *Maya* in Sanskrit, which is more complimenting to our material existence. The word *Maya* also means *magical*. This would explain how something magical can be perceived as an illusion. But magic is often ascribed to what we cannot explain, which doesn't mean that it is not real; it just means that we don't yet have a logical explanation for it.

We are creative forces, magicians who are able to imagine something and then use our different talents and capabilities to bring it into physical existence. This interpretation is much more empowering in that it removes us from living isolated in a world devoid of meaning and purpose. It plants us in fertile soil that can grow into a beautiful expression and design of the world we want to live in.

What may be an illusion is that our physical world is inanimate, devoid of any consciousness. When we see beyond the veil of this illusion, we come into contact with a living world, where everything is an intelligent field of consciousness that has organized itself into the material world with which we interact. Everything is an expression of the intention with which it was created. This is why immersing ourselves in the vast natural planes—like walking on the beach, hiking in the mountains, or sightseeing from a vast viewpoint—provides a sense of expansion and nourishment deep inside us. Likewise, sitting in a room in our home, which was designed to bring us tranquility, can promote calmness and give us a moment of respite.

On the other hand, wearing a cheaply-made outfit may look good, but its hidden design and construction inadequacies can reflect an identity gap that leaves us feeling invaluable and wanting more for ourselves. So, we try again, seeking another outfit to boost our esteem while limiting ourselves to low-cost items. It's a cycle that only drives esteem down instead of up. I'm not suggesting we excuse ourselves from buying bargains. But I am suggesting that we deserve to look and feel our best. What we wear can facilitate that or undermine it.

I spent decades wondering whether I was just not spiritually evolved enough, being so caught up in the illusion of our material world, or whether I was just unable to see beyond the misconception of conventional spiritual teachings. Today, I can confidently say that our material existence is not an illusion. Instead, we are part of an astonishing cosmic partnership. We are living on the edge of creation. We are here to bring into physical reality that which has not existed before. Look how we have created an entire civilization from what grows within and above the soil. It is beyond magical. It goes beyond words. And we all play a role—to bring forth our unique and most magnanimous desires, using our unique talents, capabilities, and tools to collaborate and create magic. We are powerful creators with gifts the world needs and is waiting for us to bring forth. But to do that, we need to shift our perspective and see ourselves as magicians, living in a world where we get to conjure up a life of beauty, joy, and fulfillment.

I invite you to practice seeing yourself as a magician, conjuring up opportunities throughout your day. As you go about your life, ask yourself, *Am I becoming more intentional with what I am experiencing when I shift to perceiving myself as a magician?* Pay attention and notice whether your magic affects people you interact with throughout your day, creating miracles and synchronistic events. When you feel more confident in your magical powers, ask the Universe to team up with you and create more magic in your life.

***What are your unique magical powers, and how can you own and express them more fully?***

# Reflection Prompt

S hifting your perspective of your world is important to heeding a shift calling you from within. If you deceive yourself instead of claiming your authenticity, then you short-change yourself and your chances for true happiness and fulfill-ment. If you believe that you are separate and alone in the world, you are less likely to make a significant shift in your life and instead remain stuck in a mode of fear, unworthiness, and survival.

On the other hand, if you shift your perspective to being part of a sacred whole, you are more likely to experience your life as filled with love and care for each other and our planet. If you realize that love is your bridge between the physical world in which you live and the non-physical realm of your soul and that your senses can serve as a gateway between these two dimensions of your existence, then you are more likely to treat yourself as a sacred expression of creation. And, if you perceive yourself as a magician, you will become more playful, conjuring up the life you want to live. Experiment with shifting

your perspective and see how it affects your daily life circumstances. You can pick any of the shifts suggested here and ask
yourself *"how will shifting my perspective change my day and
how does it answer the shift calling me to transform my life and
my world?"*

# Part VII: Shifting Your Path Onward

*"If you want something you've never had,*
*you have to do something you've never done."*

—Barbra Streisand

# Embrace Profound Simplicity

Many of the ideas put forth in this book may seem, at first, like big concepts, such as being a point of consciousness on this planet, the Principle of Physical and Non-Physical Synergy, or the notion that the purpose of life is to experience itself. At the same time, these big ideas have very tangible, down-to-earth expressions in our daily living. They can be applied to any area of our life, such as our homes, work, wealth, well-being, relationships, relation to nature, etc. The same laws and principles apply at the macro level of big ideas and the micro level of our individual lives.

To bridge between the universal and your individual life, I want to show you how I use the suggestions in this book to help clients who have come to me with practical issues like losing weight, finding a job, or dealing with a troubled relationship. Using the principles I have shared with you, my clients have been able to step into a larger version of themselves and change fundamental beliefs and ways of dealing with the challenges that have kept them stuck. By offering them an expanded framework and a guided safe container, they have discovered creative possibilities, which are unique and particular to them and their healing process. They have become whole, reconnecting to the preciousness of their life. While our lives have many dimensions, here are some key areas that make up who we are.

*Which area of your life is calling you to give it your particular attention at this time?*

# Shifting Your Home

Since the pandemic, our homes have become much more than dwellings. They are retreats from the outside world, our offices, playgrounds, and sanctuaries for our souls. I'm willing to guess we spend more time in our homes than ever before. They have become central to our existence. So, we must create an environment that serves our daily needs while reminding us of our power and purpose. We need to shift how we think of our homes from being buildings to places where we can build up ourselves. Our homes must strike a balance between where we can be productive and where we replenish ourselves. I like to envision our homes as "greenhouses" that nourish growth instead of "fortresses" that protect us from the outside world. This shift in perspective leads to a shift in our actions.

For example, we often allow clutter to pile up in our workspace, living areas, and bedrooms. It's like allowing weeds to spring up and suffocate other plant life. If we see a mess and endless to-do lists wherever we look, our senses can't find fertile soil to rest and replenish our batteries. As a result, we may overlook the mess without realizing that it affects our mood, state of mind, interactions, and clarity of our thinking. So, simply clearing our desks, decluttering a bookshelf, and cleaning up a room can begin to open our minds to creativity and opportunity. Besides, we may just find that thing we've been looking for.

Every corner of every room in our homes releases energy that can build up, tear down, soothe, or cause stress. So, by shifting our intentions, our homes can become sources of comfort, inspiration, creativity, playfulness, or any other quality with which we wish to permeate our living quarters.

Applying the principles of spiritual-material wholeness and physical and non-physical synergy, we can relate to our home environment and the objects we have collected over the years as expressions of our values, taste, memories, and aspirations.

To shift your home onward, ask, *Does my home reflect who I am and how I want to live?* Then, walk through the rooms, spending time to reflect, *How do I feel when I'm in this room? Is it what I'd like to experience when I enter this area? What can I amplify or change?* You can also ask yourself, *How can I make my home a sanctuary, a spiritually nourishing space for myself?*

Let's say you want to create a corner that inspires tranquility and comfort. Now visualize a situation, place, or thing that reminds you of that warmth, safety, and solace. Natural settings often connect me to this feeling, like sitting on a garden bench surrounded by plants and flowers as the sun's rays heat my skin. Perhaps, I'll envision a water feature, my favorite plants, and light shining through the trees to contribute to this sense of calm. How can you create more serenity in this particular corner of your home? What colors, what furniture, and objects come to mind?

I'm not necessarily recommending new furniture, although that may help, but we can give items we already have a new purpose, which inspires this "new" corner of bliss. For example, we can reconnect with familiar pieces that remind us of peaceful places, loving relationships, fond memories, or a familiar desire.

Instead of drawing inspiration from a garden setting, you may hang a portrait of your favorite family member who would rock you to sleep while singing lullabies. This memory holds the quality of comfort within it. Then every time you wish to experience some comfort and feel a calm wash over you, you can look at that image and connect to the potent sensations it evokes in you. You can see how the physical world around you can come to life and begin communicating with you, comforting you, relaxing you, or inspiring you, whichever atmosphere you decide to create in your home.

During the early days of the COVID-19 lockdown, I invited members of my online community to find many different qualities in their homes to enrich their day and find inspiration and companionship during a challenging time for us all. We didn't just pick tranquility and calm; we looked for playfulness and humor in different objects in our homes and shared what made us laugh. We found healing wisdom in the essential oils we kept in our bathrooms and used them to create different moods at different times. We found flow and rhythm in the music we listened to when we needed a break, and many more qualities, depending on what each member wanted to evoke and access for themselves.

Just like you can become a conduit for a particular quality you want to express, so can the objects that surround you. Select any quality you want to experience, such as high energy, creativity, flow, focus, wisdom, or connection. Find the objects that evoke that quality or emotion for you, and then connect with that object whenever you want to experience that desired state of mind and feeling. Remember, objects are alive and can be our allies. They hold our values, dreams, likes, and dislikes. And they hold qualities of their own based on what they are made of, their form, and their function.

This process allows our homes to come alive with any mood, emotion, or qualities of which we want more. Want productivity? Create a space that focuses your attention. Want more love? Find things, places, and people you love and create a space for them in your home. Want creativity? Find objects that inspire you. Want a stress-free zone? Surround yourself with relaxing images or comfortable furniture. Create spaces for anything that shifts your perception of yourself, perspective of the world, and probability for success. Then use objects that connect you to the qualities that awaken this purpose in you.

Your home can become an expression of your unique personality, the functions you desire, and your particular life circumstances. And it can also become a vibrant expression of emotional states you wish to enhance and a sanctuary to increase and strengthen your spiritual connection. Instead of

waiting for the next opportunity to go on a retreat or a reju-
venating vacation, turn your residence into your physical and
spiritual home.

The more you practice, the more readily available these
states of mind and emotion will become. The more you practice, the more enjoyment you will experience in spending time
in your home environment, and the more you will feel fulfilled
with what you have, as your relationship with the objects in
your home will enrich you. You will find that your urge to
acquire more things will diminish as you find greater enjoyment and fulfillment in what you already own and have brought
to life. Your home can become your haven, spiritual retreat
center, sense of connection, and a place to nurture growth—
your greenhouse.

*How can you bring alive the environment of your home and
make it a greenhouse that nurtures growth?*

# Shifting Your Work

Most of us have to work for a living, but we don't always find meaning and purpose in our work. We envy those we imagine have found purpose in selfless service to others, like a doctor or a teacher, or those with a special gift or talent and a clear career path, like a musician or an athlete. But what about all the rest of us who were not born with a clear calling or an exceptional talent? Don't we deserve to find purpose in our primary occupation, as well?

Here are three common misconceptions about finding your life purpose and how to turn them around and make your purpose matter—making it count and making it practical and real.

**The first misconception** is believing your life purpose is waiting for you, and you just haven't stumbled upon it yet. This can mess with you because it means that you must keep looking for this special and fulfilling occupation that is somewhere out there in the distant future. But what if you don't find it? What if you miss it and live the rest of your life wondering where you might have gone wrong? And what if it takes decades until you find it? What are you supposed to be doing until then? Just work to pay bills without any meaning and purpose to your existence? It sounds soul-crushing.

Consider instead that your life purpose is composed of two dimensions: a spiritual essence and a multitude of material expressions that this essence can take at different times, depending on your circumstances.

The spiritual essence of your calling is a quality you identify as essential to who you are. When you lead with this quality and express it in your daily interactions, you are naturally filled with a satisfying sense of meaning and purpose. This essence is usually a word or two or a short expression that summarizes who you are at your core. It is not a mission statement of what you do in the world but rather the essence of your soul, described at a high level in just a few words. Ask yourself, *What quality am I supposed to share with the world?*

This is a new way of looking at your life purpose. I invite you to begin with an internal shift that will become an external change. So, instead of searching for this big life purpose, go inward and ask yourself, *What makes me come alive? What do I feel passionate about? What makes me feel whole? What makes me feel fulfilled? What brings me a sense of balance?* Then look at what stands out to you from everything you have realized about yourself, or look at a common theme in your responses to these questions. That which will emerge is the spiritual essence of your calling. And if you want to take this a step further, apply the Principle of Physical and Non-Physical Synergy and imagine what this essence feels like and looks like. Then, have an internal dialogue between this essence and yourself and discover valuable insights to help you find more meaning and purpose in your life.

Here are a few examples of what people have discovered about the essence of their calling when I've led them through a simple-guided exercise, much like the questions I've asked you above.

- A retired businessman discovered that the essence of his calling was "clarity and direction." He always felt crystal clear when deciding which direction to take in his business. That's when he felt most alive and what made him very successful.
- A woman I worked with was in between jobs and wondered what type of job to look for. She identified the essence of her life purpose as being a "mother goose." She had always loved being a mom and was often labeled "mother goose" by her younger colleagues. Realizing the essence of who she was and what made her most happy allowed her to look for a job where she could mentor younger team members and find deep fulfillment at work.
- Other examples of what people have identified as the essence of their life purpose are: being curious about the world, spiritual-material abundance, creative expression, high performance, thinking out of the box, connection and community, and many more.

This is a new way of perceiving who you are and what will bring you meaning and purpose. These might sound like just words when you read them here on the page, but when you find your word or phrase, you will feel that you have nailed the essence of who you are and what you have to offer your world, and I know it will make you very happy.

**The second common misconception** about our life purpose is that it must rely on a specific occupation. I invite you to expand that perspective on your life purpose and consider that the material expression of your calling reflects your spiritual essence and can take many different forms of expression. You see, the material dimension of your calling consists of the different areas of your life where you can express this essence. There are many, such as at work, at home, with your family and friends, in your community, in your self-care, health, and in your relationship with money. As we are talking about the essence of who you are, it makes sense that it is not limited to the hours you spend at work but includes every interaction you have, every decision you make, and every action you take throughout your day. When you align the spiritual essence of who you are with everything material and physical you do, you tap into your passion and experience deep fulfillment and immense satisfaction from experiencing such spiritual-material wholeness. In fact, you increase your probability of fully embracing the purpose of life and experiencing yourself more fully. You get to feel connected to your divine essence because you are connected to what you were meant to share with your world. Now, with the spiritual and material dimensions of your life purpose available to you, there is one more common misconception I want you to consider.

**The third misconception** may sound like this, *My life purpose is only truly meaningful when it focuses on being of service to others*. While it sounds noble, this will lead to fatigue, disappointment, and frustration. Instead, you must be mindful of being of service to yourself first. I don't mean selfishly, but rather like putting on an oxygen mask in an airplane emergency before you try to save others. This allows you to express the spiritual essence of your life's calling in everything you do, aligning you to your highest purpose, which will increase the flow of vitality in you and will serve others in the process.

If you discover the quality which is at the essence of who you are, and express this quality in everything you do, then you get to live with purpose and do good in the world at the same time. Because the truth is that there is such rich diversity in each of us expressing the essence of who we are as we serve others. I offer you one of my favorite quotes by Howard Thurman that speaks precisely to serving the world by fully living the essence of your life's purpose. "Don't ask what the world needs. Ask what makes you come alive and go do it, because what the world needs are people who have come alive."

*How can you express your unique gifts and talents more fully in your private and professional life?*

# Shifting Your Wealth

On the one hand, we are told that money can't bring us happiness, and on the other hand, many of us believe that having more money will bring us the freedom to do less of what we have to do and more of what we want to do and, therefore, will make us happier. Confusing, don't you think? How can money be both something we don't want to be seen with in public and, at the same time, the secret we most long for to fulfill our big dreams? My father used to say that money can't make you happy, but it can make your misery more comfortable. What is your relationship to money? Do you love it or hate it?

It makes sense that we would feel frustrated and even bitter at not having enough money if we believe that only when we'll have more of it will we be able to fulfill some of what we most long for. After all, our dreams are an extension of who we are at our core, and so feeling that who we are can only happen at some future time when we'll have enough money for it can be devastating. This train of thought implies that we can only be partially who we are now and must wait to become more fully ourselves at some uncertain future time. And, maybe, we'll never get to live our lives to their fullest because right now, money can only serve to pay our bills, and fulfilling our dream is a luxury we can't currently afford. And then we feel that we should not expect that much from money as we are told that money alone will not make us happy. Many of us might not even be aware of our ambivalent relationship with money, but it is present in our culture and upbringing and can be soul-crushing.

Money is a powerful energy. It can offer us basic needs and rights, including food, shelter, and healthcare. It can allow us to express ourselves more fully in the world and promote causes dear to us. So, of course, we expect money to be available to us in abundance, as it has the potential to cater to all our needs. But here's where we miss the point. Too often, we focus on the amount of money we have in the bank as if it is the only proof that our dreams will come true. Actually, what most of us want are the qualities and experiences that we believe money can afford us. We wish to experience more freedom, ease, abundance, playfulness, creative self-expression, time with friends, a greater sense of community, and so on. Now, I'm sure you would agree that there are many different ways to respond to these needs that don't involve money.

That's where wealth comes in. You see, this entire conversation has been about shifting your perspective on money and perceiving the potential of real wealth that is always available to you. For example, if you long to experience a wealth of freedom in your life, how can you do that regardless of the amount of money you have? Time is one way to have more freedom, but there are other ways to experience this quality. What would

                                   Shift Calling

make your spirit feel free? The money will follow if it needs to once you focus on experiencing more freedom in your life.

If you want money to be more generous, become more generous yourself. Ask yourself, *How can I tap into a wealth of generosity within myself?* Evaluate your responses and start expressing the wealth you seek. You will find yourself surrounded by generosity, giving and receiving more of it.

Focusing on wealth allows you to connect to the emotional and spiritual qualities you seek to increase. Money is one answer, but there are many more creative solutions to what you seek. Focusing on increasing the wealth in your life instead of the money you have will increase your probability of experiencing abundance and prosperity. Take one step at a time. Pick one area in your life, one intention you can identify, followed by one action you can take to increase your wealth in this domain. Then celebrate the shift in your perception of yourself and your perspective of your world as a result of your actions. Enjoy the wealth you already have and the wealth coming your way. Always remember that the richness you have in any area of your life is your prosperity.

And as for shifting our relationship with money, rather than cringing at the thought of talking openly about loving money and what it affords us, let's develop a loving relationship with money. Let's treat money like the powerful force that it is and develop an ongoing channel of communication with it. Applying the Principle of Physical and Non-Physical Synergy can be a useful tool in shifting our relationship for the better.

For example, when I work with a client on their relationship with money, I take them through an exercise where I ask them to list the traits of their ideal romantic lover. Then, at the end of the guided exercise, I ask them whether they can relate these traits to their relationship to money. Most clients are surprised by how much they neglect their relationship with money because of this ambiguous relationship of not wanting to talk openly about loving money and what it can afford them and yet, expecting money to deliver them freedom, abundance, and happiness. It can be kind of crazy-making, and yet, people are often unable to untangle this relationship because, to do that, they'd have to admit to themselves, and maybe even others, that they love money and want to have more of it.

Another way to befriend money is to complete the sentence: My prosperity serves the world by _________________. How would you complete this sentence? In what ways does being prosperous serve the world you live in? It is a question that invites you into a more expansive version of yourself, the possibility of living your life more fully and finding meaning and purpose in what you do and who you are. So, give yourself some time to reflect on how your prosperity could serve you and the world around you. You could imagine how it would serve your work in the world, your relationships, your health and well-being, and how you may want to increase your impact. Allow yourself to have fun with this. Dream big. Take risks. Come alive. Money is just a vehicle for living life more fully and serving the world in a bigger and more generous way.

*In what area of your life would you like to increase your wealth, and how can you go about doing it?*

# Shifting Your Well-Being

Wellness is usually associated with the pursuit of physical health, like diet and nutrition, sleep, fitness, relaxation, and so on. But well-being goes beyond physical health, encompassing your full being, which includes your physical and spiritual wellness and any other dimension of your life, such as finding meaning in your work, mental and emotional wellness, and social and economic wellness. During these intense times of planetary turmoil, the scope of what is included in our well-being keeps expanding.

If you think about it, well-being comes from growing into a larger, more expansive version of yourself. For example, you may have started exercising and increasing your flexibility. Perhaps you are experiencing more joy and focus throughout your day due to committing to a regular meditation practice. You may have decided to step out of your comfort zone and try to make a living doing what you are passionate about. Or you may have expanded your sense of purpose and belonging within a social or activist group. In these examples, expanding the range of your actions and emotions improves your condition, creating a new balance between your aspirations and perceived results. This gives you an uplifting feeling of well-being.

Whatever area of well-being you wish to focus on, there is usually a goal you are aiming for. What you envision yourself aiming for is usually inspired by that part of you that aspires to become your best and most fulfilled self, your *inner ideal-self*. That is the part that wants you to keep growing and improve your internal feeling of well-being and your external conditions. But then comes the *sabotaging-self*, reminding you how hard it is to make a change, encouraging you to quit. This is the part that is most often driven by a wound or a trauma. This part has usually developed to protect you from a painful situation where you didn't have the tools to deal with your life situation and instead developed a coping mechanism that probably saved you at the time. It may not serve you well anymore, but the sabotaging-self keeps undermining any attempt to expand your well-being.

And so, you find yourself in an internal battle between your ideal-self and sabotaging-self. This often expresses itself in attempts to improve your well-being, followed by one failed attempt after another, because this sabotaging part just shows up each time and stops any genuine effort at moving onward. This can be disheartening and cause you to lose confidence in your ability to make a real change. I have found that it can build up self-hatred as you become disappointed in yourself for failing.

This was exactly the case with a client of mine who came to me to work specifically on losing weight. She was suffering from different physical ailments because she was overweight.

When we began working together, she was desperate to reach her goal and felt ashamed for all her failed attempts. I invited her to let go of the need for an external result of losing a specific amount of weight. Instead, we explored internal shifts she could make that would prove more effective, including a third part inside of her that can manage her eating habits, giving space for success or setbacks. The loving, nurturing part within her was able to explain the internal battle and identify what was triggering and activating each part. This third part was able to help change her relationship with how she nourished herself. I call this your *nurturing-self.*

We each have the internal ideal self, the sabotaging self, and the nurturing self. Whichever issue you focus on, you'll find these parts are present. It can be very empowering and liberating to know that each of these parts is a living aspect of you that you can dialogue with and gain insight into your particular situation. Applying the Principle of Physical and Non-Physical Synergy, you can engage in a dialogue with any or all of these three parts within you. You will gain such insight and wisdom into your situation and discover empowering creative solutions that will shift your trajectory onward.

You can do this with any issue you want to work on regarding your well-being, whether your entry point is primarily physical, emotional, mental, spiritual, social, or any other issue in your life. Invite your ideal-self, sabotaging-self, and nurturing-self to a constructive and collaborative dialogue. Treat your inner parts as living beings with needs, desires, and unique life stories. Let each part speak in its turn so you can understand what drives it and how it can help you make an internal shift resulting in external change and an increased sense of well-being. Pay attention to your ideal-self. Honor this part that wants you to become the best version of yourself. It is the part that wants you to shift onward.

Then bring in the part that is sabotaging any good attempt of yours. This part protected you earlier when you didn't have the tools to deal with the pain and suffering you experienced. This part offered protection in the best way possible, using whatever means were available to you then. Converse with it and get to know why it is continuing to protect you in ways that are not useful anymore. What message does it want to convey to you?

Acknowledge that both these parts are your shift calling to transform your life, with a promise of what's possible and a disruption that reminds you that your current ways are not working anymore. Finally, gain wisdom from your nurturing-self, which can strike a mutually beneficial deal for your well-being. These parts are your sacred allies in helping you shift your path onward. Expanding your field of information by including all the players involved—each with their unique needs and wisdom—holds the promise of empowering and life-affirming solutions.

I remind you that you are a portal between the physical and non-physical, the spiritual and the material. You can imagine something and bring it into existence. And then, you can become the conduit of what you have imagined and express it in your daily living. So, I invite you to envision the new, nurturing part, as I shared earlier in Part VI when I was working with an early memory as a newborn. It was the love and nurturing of my imaginary Black Panther tribe of women that healed me. So, bring in an idealized mother or father figure or a mentor or guardian angel—whomever you want to bring in as your ideal caregiver. Bring this part to life and give it the traits you most long for to support, guide, and love you.

Then ask how it can help you resolve your ongoing battle between your sabotaging-self and your inner ideal-self. Know that your thoughts will organize into unique and wise options that will give you the best guidance to transform your situation. The information you will receive will not be something you would have thought of before on your own. Instead, this new internal part will provide you with a new conscious awareness of moving forward with your situation in the most caring and effective way. It is pretty magical that you can create a nurturing part within you because it means you don't have to be defined by your past. You can reimagine your present and future and become a conduit for this new reality. That is living life on the edge of creation and creating the conditions to live your life more fully, which will give you a greater sense of meaning, purpose, and a profound sense of well-being. Try it and see what happens.

My client's breakthrough happened in one of our sessions when she saw her inner ideal-self standing behind a closed door and refusing to come out. It told her that she allowed her sabotaging-self to rule how she nourished herself. This part assured her it would come out once she nurtured herself more regularly with the new mother she had created. The message was clear and simple. My client realized that she had to mother herself if she wanted to be free of excess eating. She began listening to the daily guidance of her ideal nurturing mother and practiced small acts of loving kindness toward herself. She nourished herself like she had never been nourished by gaining insight and guidance from an internal, imaginary, nurturing mother.

Ultimately, it is self-love that will heal your wounds and stop your inner battles. It is self-love that will shift your path onward. And it is by engaging in a dialogue with all the inner parts involved in the issue with which you are dealing, and relating to each one of them as insightful, non-physical aspects of yourself, that you will accelerate your spiritual growth and increase your probabilities for transformation.

*What area of your life would you like to nurture more intentionally so that you can increase your sense of well-being?*

# Shifting Your Relationships

Our closest and dearest relationships are often the most challenging, as they come with varying degrees of demands and bring out parts in us that we don't always like about ourselves. What if we can shift our perspective beyond the typical labels of spouse, child, parent, colleague, or acquaintance and instead perceive the different people with whom we engage as our spiritual teachers? This doesn't mean we put everyone on a pedestal to worship. Rather, we envision every encounter as an opportunity to heal and grow on our quest to become whole human beings.

If we apply the principles suggested in this book, we can expand our perceptions of our loved ones and experience them as allies that can help us grow into the best version of ourselves. Take, for example, seemingly random encounters with strangers. We often perceive those as synchronistic gifts that appeared just at the right time, delivering a much-needed message that can even be life-changing. What if we could experience our regular and closest relationships similarly, only more so, as our residential spiritual teachers?

While random strangers come and go, which makes it easier to perceive the gift in our encounter with them, our closest relationships are also significant in our lives because they offer us the opportunity to grow and change over time. They usually stay with us through thick and thin and allow us to take our time to make the necessary shifts in our perception of ourselves and our perspective of the world. They allow us to find our way in our own timing and transform ourselves and our lives for the better. But that's not always how we perceive many of our closest connections. So, let's examine a few of these primary relationships and see how we can shift our experience of them by incorporating the spiritual dimension of our connection. This doesn't mean bypassing the challenges we face with them, but rather, seeing our connection from a place of love and appreciation for the gifts they offer. And, yes, some relationships offer forms of unconditional love, while others teach us about the pain and suffering of conditional love. Either way, we learn about what works and doesn't work for us, what brings us closer to the joy of being connected to our inner divinity, and what takes us away from this connection and makes us miserable.

Practicing the Principle of Spiritual-Material Wholeness can be very helpful here. For example, let's take our parents, who brought us into this world. Some of us have nurturing and supportive relationships with our parents, but many of us find these relationships challenging. When the latter occurs, we often reject everything about this relationship as we try to find our identity and separate from what we don't like about our parents. But instead, you can think of what gifts your parents have passed on to you rather than focusing on what you dislike about them. Shifting your focus will connect you to the love that flows between you in the higher, spiritual realms, at a soul level.

For example, a woman I worked with never liked her mother's taste and how she decorated my client's childhood home. After engaging in a guided exercise that focused on the spiritual gifts we received from our parents, my client realized that she had inherited from her mother her sense of aesthetics and attention to detail. Suddenly, she was able appreciate the spiritual gifts her mother had given her. Instead of focusing on hating her mother's particular taste and how she had expressed this gift of attention to aesthetics and detail, she could now feel a deep connection to her mother and to what they shared.

As she went through the same exercise focused on the spiritual gifts we received from our parents, a young woman I worked with realized that she shared a sense of curiosity and adventure with her estranged father, which allowed her to connect with how much she had loved him as a child when they traveled as a family.

You can see how focusing on the spiritual gifts you received from your parents doesn't take away the hurt that happened or personality differences, but it allows you to focus on the gifts that have been passed on to you. Focusing on such spiritual gifts opens up the channels for these gifts to flow more freely from your parents to you. Focusing on the spiritual dimension of the relationship allows you to connect to the love that exists on a heart level. Remember, you wouldn't find your relationships challenging if you didn't care much about the people you perceive as having hurt you.

If we look at our romantic relationships, we will find that we often choose the person who takes us back to unresolved patterns from our youth. At the same time, that person often holds the key to our liberation. If we stick around long enough and don't divorce at the first challenge, we discover that our life partners are, unbeknownst to them, our primary spiritual guides. They bear potential gifts of liberation and freedom from our childhood wounds if we are willing to work through the challenges and claim our power in the relationship. So, ask yourself, *What potential spiritual gifts are in store with my romantic partner?* Whatever particular response comes to you, know that the intimacy of a romantic relationship holds great promise. Sometimes the promise is given without effort, while other times, you must claim it as part of your self-empowerment.

I often say that I have been very lucky in my relationship with my spouse, but I've worked hard to be so lucky. My spouse and I discovered, early in our relationship, that we shared a wound of not being fully seen by our parents. Many people don't feel seen by their parents or teachers. It can be devastating. In romantic relationships, we often expect our partner to heal us from our core wounds. Instead, what often happens is that our partner just continues opening up that old wound. So it takes much inner introspection to work through such core patterns in a relationship. If you take the journey, the rewards are well worth the pain. My spouse and I have held each other in our most vulnerable moments and witnessed our individual transformation. And as a result, we have become more compassionate human beings.

Likewise, our children seem to know exactly what buttons to press to trigger us. How do they know what issues we have to work on to grow as human beings and parents? Well, I believe our children are our spiritual teachers, and we, their earthly guides. The gift our children offer us, as their parents, is the opportunity to relive our childhood, only this time as able and independent adults. And while we each have a unique story that we get to revisit through our children, if we perceive our children as having wisdom to share, we can pay attention to what they are teaching us. We can acknowledge their gift of unconditional love, which helps us heal from the lack we might have experienced the first time around. In return, our job is to be earthly guides to our children, showing them how to stay connected to their divine inner being as they negotiate life on our sometimes very challenging planet.

For example, I was terrified of my father's raging fits and occasional beatings as a child. I was told that my father's father would get so angry at my father when he was a kid that he would beat him with a belt. So, I grew up easily losing my temper. When I became a mother, I had done enough personal work that I knew I wanted to change this pattern. I began looking for alternative responses to my anger, as I didn't want my children to experience the terror I had experienced as a child. I also learned how to manage my kids' anger without shutting down. My infinite love for them allowed me and my family to shift this destructive generational pattern.

All relationships hold the promise of healing and growth, even those that may seem, from the outside, less intense. Work colleagues become our teachers in the area of our work and self-expression in the world, and our friends teach us different lessons about staying connected and true to ourselves in the presence of another.

Regardless of the relationship, the people we encounter in our lifetime offer us gifts of learning and growth. For some of us, these lessons are more intense than for others, but no one escapes having to grow their soul, let go of unnecessary pain, and create healing in their life.

If looked upon from an expanded spiritual perspective or purely energetic perspective, when two entities of conscious intelligence meet, their unique vibrations bump against each other. In this process, they discover whether there is a possibility for a creative connection that will bear the fruit of something new and fresh. This is the case when two different atoms connect, like hydrogen and oxygen creating water for life to thrive. The same is the case when two people meet and decide to build a connection. The more aware we become of the spiritual potential in our relationships, the more fruitful they can become, and the more they can be a source of love in our world.

***Which relationship would you like to reevaluate and deepen, and what is the first step you would like to take?***

# Shifting Your Relationship to Nature

I parked the car and walked toward the designated entrance. Three poles created a simple arc that seemed to command a moment of mindfulness before walking into the woods. The carving at the top read "Grove of the Old Trees." I walked through the arc into a thick grove of redwood trees. The ground was mostly flat and covered with large ferns. The path was windy and marked by branches that had been laid down on both sides. Magnificent tall redwoods greeted me on both sides as I found my way to an open sitting area with a few tables and benches. A young couple walked by with a toddler that ran before them, squealing with delight. I thought to myself, *the trees must love when children come to visit them and express sheer joy in their presence.*

I looked around and found a flat area where I could lie on the ground, looking up at a group of redwoods surrounding me. I closed my eyes and breathed deeply for a few minutes. I began noticing birds chirping. As I lay there quieting my mind, their singing intensified and grew louder. I looked up at the tall trees above me and marveled at their peaceful and majestic presence.

I wondered how trees felt about us cutting them down for our human needs, to provide fire and build furniture, houses, boats, and railway tracks. An unexpected answer came back from what I can only assume was the consciousness of the redwood trees surrounding me. The response had this quality, which I had come to recognize over the years, of telepathic communication with an aspect of nature's consciousness. A physical and non-physical synergy. At such times, I was always relaxed and open, feeling joy or appreciation for my natural surroundings. In this case, it was not my voice speaking back to me but a different quality of communication that commanded my attention.

A sense of joy came over me, and to my surprise, I heard the words, "We offer ourselves to humans. It is part of our sacred bond. We enjoy being used for your creative living. That is part of our shared destiny. But you keep taking without replenishing and restoring balance, without a thought for the future or any consideration of the entire ecosystems we host. You do not consider what we need to keep thriving. Don't just take without a thought about the future, as it is our collective future. Let us restore the sacred bond between us and regain the balance we have lost."

This is one example among many where I have had internal communication with what I call the consciousness of nature. My personal experience and that of working with others has shown me that when we find ourselves in nature and melt into it, we gain access to invaluable wisdom which can help us in our particular situation and on a more global and collective level. These types of communications embody an expansive quality, a tapping into the spiritual-material wholeness of life, and an inner communication between the physical and the non-physical. They also offer a fuller experience of our world and a greater sense of meaning and purpose.

Many years ago, as part of my dissertation research, I led workshops on my property and would send participants out into the garden to find answers to the issues present for them during the workshop. I told them to visit different corners of the garden and take in the scents, views, and overall feeling in each corner. They were asked to remain silent and take it all in. It was remarkable to hear the insights with which they returned.

One participant found herself standing by a cluster of trees where the branches of two trees touched each other at certain points. Her focus for that workshop related to issues of selfhood and boundaries, and she realized the trees were showing her how to balance her sense of self with gentle interactions with others. It was a profound insight and one that was unique to her. While all the participants of my workshops visited the same cluster of trees, only this particular participant found the trees showing her how to stand in her power and have healthy interaction with others.

Two other participants were drawn to different ants' nests in the sand and spent some time studying them. One participant found herself reframing her usual resentment about how hard her life was as she saw the ants just getting on with their life without complaining all the time. Their industriousness humbled her, giving her a renewed perspective on her life. The other participant was more focused on how the ants worked together, reminding her of the value of collaborating instead of doing everything on her own. So, even two participants in different workshops who each spent time watching ants had different insights about their lives.

In this way, nature is a great healer and teacher. We must take the time to slow down, take in nature, blend with it, and trust the meaning that arises in the moment. This is the power of attuning to nature. Each one of these participants had profound insights. An encounter with a colony of ants or visiting a cluster of trees offered each participant exactly the insight she needed at that moment.

If you don't have easy access to nature, you can even look at images of nature on a digital device. During lockdown, I would take workshop participants through a guided meditation online with their eyes wide open, looking at stunning images of nature. My goal was to provide a gateway to an expansive, blissful state of being. Participants were amazed at how high they felt at the end of the guided meditation, even though it was a virtual experience of nature and not a walk outdoors in nature or a traditional guided meditation with soft music and closed eyes.

Try doing this for yourself. Pick stunning pictures of nature from the internet that evoke different emotions in you. Then go through the different images you picked and take a moment to look at each one. Stay with it briefly, and then move on to the next image. You will find that each image awakens a different part of you. Just five minutes of this exercise will improve your mood.

I began by sharing with you a message I got from the redwoods in a grove of old trees. But I also got a profound message from a small house plant during the early days of the COVID lockdown. And the participants in my workshops have all had meaningful insight from spending quiet time in nature or through a digital slideshow of stunning photos of nature. Don't limit yourself to one way or another, and don't compare yourself to any examples I've shared. Just make your own connection with nature, ask for guidance, and trust what emerges in the moment. Nature is a powerful living consciousness with which we can engage and collaborate, and it can be an important teacher and ally.

*How can you deepen your relationship with nature through either outdoor activities or inward communication?*

# Shifting Your Global Impact

Spiritual teacher Esther Hicks says that one person who is connected to Source energy, or God, if you prefer, is more powerful than one million who are not connected. I'm sure you have experienced the power of being swept away by someone's conviction and have had your heart cracked wide open as they speak from their authentic self and share their fervor. A connection with Source can inspire us to step up and become more authentic, care more for the plight of others, and champion a cause important to us. It ignites our fire with spiritual fuel and gives us a purpose beyond our personal stories and circumstances. It makes us feel connected to something bigger and promises a better life for ourselves and others. We just have to be careful that the means to this promise are not at the expense of other people or other species.

Revisiting each of the principles and suggestions in this book will connect you to your unique essence, ignite your spiritual fire, and increase your agency and, consequently, your global reach and impact. While you may have connected more with certain suggestions over others, here are some reminders that I find especially potent in fueling your fire and getting you engaged and impactful in the world around you.

Start with my "big picture" theme to live from the spiritual essence of your life purpose. When you express your authentic essence, you are at your optimal state, which will increase your impact. Become a conduit for what makes you come alive, and you will set the people around you on fire.

You are also a pollinator and can inspire others to become more of who they truly are, just like they see you are doing. And, you never know how you will awaken the fire in others and how others will pass on the torch and ignite still more. Practicing being a conduit for good in the world, whatever it may be for you, is a potent way to spread your presence more effectively. When you operate as a conduit for connection to the sacredness of life and the causes you care deeply about, in whatever way you choose to do that, then whomever you are in contact with throughout your day gets to bask in your presence. The particular field that you are emanating will rub off on them and make them feel more inspired and fully engaged in life.

It may take practice to become a powerful, intentional presence, but keep training and increasing your agency and influence. This is your personal work and spiritual practice. And ultimately, your personal work is spiritual work, and your spiritual work is world work. Your actions may seem small and insignificant unless you hold a perspective of thinking globally while acting locally. Keep a global perspective in your intention and awareness while effectuating one-degree shifts in yourself and influencing those in your immediate surroundings.

In Part I, I shared about homeschooling my children and feeling that I was on the cutting edge of child education and making a difference through our family's small and local actions. It was not the baking activity or Lego play that increased our impact in the world. Still, the process radically shifted my perspective on how meaningful learning can occur outside the classroom. It was by deconstructing common beliefs about education and adapting new and more life-affirming ones that I felt I was thinking globally while acting locally, and where I felt that my personal work was world work and tipped the balance toward a better world for our children. And as a pollinator, other people in my social circles began homeschooling because it spoke to what they wanted for their children, as well.

Likewise, you can turn your personal work into global work by applying an expansive intention and examine underlying beliefs and perspectives that may keep you small and stuck. There's a line in the Disney movie *Mulan* where the emperor says to his commander, "A single grain of rice can tip the scale." In the movie, Mulan was the difference that tipped the scale from defeat to victory. You have the same power as a single grain of rice that can make a difference and better our world.

For example, if you are working through relationship issues with your life partner, imagine yourself transforming issues around gender or how to deal with sexuality in our culture. Use your situation to examine how it relates to prevalent customs and decide what works for you and what you need to change. Then take a risk and make the change. It will liberate a huge amount of pent-up energy and allow you to come alive.

In the same way, when you are dealing with your physical or mental well-being, your particular situation is influenced by prevalent cultural messages, societal norms, and social pressures that constrict you, one way or another. By adopting an expansive perspective, you can look at all of these and decide what you want to keep and what you want to let go of. When you do that, you liberate yourself and tip the scales toward better conditions for humanity.

If you want to improve your working conditions and experience more meaning and purpose in your professional life, then imagine how you are inspiring people around you to dare do the same. When you take a big risk, you better the working conditions for our world, even if indirectly, because you have decided to dream big and come alive. Of course, you might not see the results immediately, but be of strong faith that you are part of a tidal wave that is made up of singular drops.

Finally, collaboration can shift your impact on the world. I love the anthropologist Margaret Mead's quote, "Don't underestimate the power of a small group of committed people to change the world. In fact, it's the only thing that ever has."

I'm amazed each time I search for something obscure on the internet to find that there is information out there about anything you want. Someone has created a website, a non-profit, or another opportunity to serve those interested in the same topic. It truly is a world wide web of connections. There are people out there who are interested in what you are interested in. Some people are dealing with the same issues and suffering from the same ailment as you. And some people share the same dreams as you do. You can shift your impact on the world by joining forces.

I worked with a client who was legally blind and wanted to share her story with the world. Messages of failure haunted her since her childhood. Now that she was retired, she decided to set herself the goal of mastering different physical challenges over the span of a year to prove to herself that she could succeed despite her disability. I found her story so inspiring that we created a guided workbook that she could promote and share with anyone who wanted to prove to themselves that they could succeed as she had.

Collaborating becomes more fruitful and enjoyable when you practice the following three Cs: Compassion, Collaboration, and Creativity. When practicing compassion, you are expanding your awareness to take in the experience and perspective of others while also allowing your viewpoint and needs to be acknowledged and met. It is a powerful practice that allows for collaboration to flow more freely. And that always breeds inclusive, life-affirming, and empowering creative solutions.

When you add to that by applying the Principle of Physical and Non-Physical Synergy, you bring into your collaboration the unseen, inner realms of consciousness. This may include the consciousness of money when dealing with financial issues, the consciousness of the land or your home when dealing with issues relating to your living situation, and so on. You can begin to appreciate how potent your collaborations will become as you include more stakeholders in your process, enabling you to shift your impact toward sustainable transformation. And that is how you engage and stay "connected to Source energy," how you "become the grain of rice that can tip the scale," and how a small group of dedicated beings, physical and non-physical, can change the world."

*If you knew you couldn't fail, how would you like to increase your impact in the world?*

# Reflection Prompt

You now have a sense of how you can apply the different shifts suggested throughout this book to any issue you are dealing with in any area of your life. You saw how I picked a principle or other suggested shift and applied it to different issues we all deal with in our personal and professional lives. You can try anything I've suggested, but make the process your own. For example, how would you shift your home and enliven your living and working environment? Pick one small shift you want to make in your home. Then, apply one suggestion from this part or another part of the book, and see how it affects other aspects of your life.

Do the same with any other area of your life, whether it be shifting your work, wealth, well-being, or impact on the world. Decide on one shift you want to experience. Then pick one of the principles from this book and decide how you will practice it to alter your life situation. Keep it simple, one desired shift at a time, one suggested practice at a time. Then, allow yourself to slowly be transformed by the shift in how you perceive yourself and your perspective of the situation. Use the principles in Part IV to help you make a one-degree shift toward a more favorable destination. You will find the compounding effect very rewarding as you shift your path onward.

# Epilogue


*"Travelers, there is no path,
paths are made by walking."*

—Antonio Machado

# Shifting Your Expectations

I believe I was put to the test during the writing of this book to see if I would stand by my own words and be open to shifting my perception of myself and my perspective on the world around me. All the ongoing work I had done throughout the years wasn't enough. The universe threw me some serious circumstances, inviting me to do some of my most profound inner work in the midst of writing. At times, I felt it slowed down my writing, and I wished it would go away. It also made me doubt the legitimacy of my recommendations when I was going through such painful processes myself. And, yet, looking back at the last six months of birthing this book, I can say that I have done some profound shifting.

As I revisited painful memories from my childhood while writing some of my personal stories, I was able to get real about what I have been sharing with you in these pages. Early in the writing, I got COVID, followed by long COVID, forcing me to look at a core pattern in my relationships. The lingering physical symptoms seemed to correspond with an old pattern of self-doubt and self-hatred that I have carried throughout my life. In addition, my 95-year-old mother was transitioning to the other side. And so I was experiencing anticipatory grief as I revisited my relationship with her over the years. I also felt that I was doing deep work on her behalf, acknowledging the suffering she had gone through, the pain I had caused her, and the traumas I had experienced in my early years. It was not easy, but it also felt very liberating. When she passed away four months into my writing, I was at peace with her and much of my childhood.

In the process, I got more insight into how trauma lives on for decades and how to rewrite our stories and liberate ourselves by shifting for the better. I experienced the power of shifting my perception of myself and my perspective on my life, as well as the compounding effect of small shifts over time.

I didn't expect to go through all this while writing my book. Instead, I had imagined myself super focused on writing down all the suggestions I wanted to share with you, the reader. Luckily, I caught on early that I was going through my own shifts amid a very focused writing period. I won't lie. It did throw me off at times, as it didn't coincide with my expectations of how the writing process would go. But, I feel more whole for taking the time to do my inner work.

Remember to pay attention to your expectations and don't let them disappoint you. Instead, open up to what the universe is offering you, what it is calling you to shift.

The only expectation I want you to have is that *You Got This!*

Other than that, watch your expectations, as they may hinder you from shifting onward. Why? Because you will be

　　　　　　　　　　　　　　　Shift Calling

focused on what you are expecting rather than on all the miracles and magic that will show up in your life once you choose to listen and act upon the shift calling you.

The more ease you bring into the process, the faster you can release what's holding you back. Remember that your divine essence is looking forward to your transformation. It longs to reunite with you more fully and continually sends you love.

The shift calling you is your ally. The circumstances you find yourself in, and the resulting emotional state you experience, call you to expand your world and know your divine essence more fully. Your shift calling is disguised in seemingly mundane troubles that appear devoid of loving purpose and precious meaning. Your work is to reconnect what you're dealing with to its divine Source, so it can shine with love and express its wholeness. So, you are never alone, whatever you are dealing with. You have your part to play, which no one can do for you. But remember that you are held in a web of life ready to shower you with more love as soon as you open up and let it in. So, let the loving flow of creation move through you!

# Acknowledgments

My deep gratitude to everyone who contributed to bringing this book into being, both my inner and outer collaborators. Thank you to the people in my life, the friends and clients I've worked with over the years who have helped refine my work. Thank you, Donna Galassi and KN Literary Arts, for your professional supervision. Thank you, David Jahr, for the literary guidance and emotional support throughout the writing process. This book would not have been written without your tireless presence. Thank you, Sarina Northway, Laura Hartley, and my beloved spouse, Leon Segal, for enthusiastically reading early drafts of the manuscript and giving me valuable feedback. In addition, I want to thank you, Leon, for supporting me during the six months of focused writing. Thank you, Lia Ottaviano, for your diligent and professional editing.

Finally, to my mother, who transitioned to the other side while I was writing this book. Thank you for nurturing in me, over the years, an appreciation for beauty, both in nature and in human craftsmanship. It has provided me the doorway to the hidden spiritual dimension of our existence and allowed me to gain profound insight into the workings of our universe.

# About Anna Gatmon, PhD

From Supermodel to Modern Mystic: Anna Gatmon, Ph.D., once graced the pages of fashion magazines and the runways for Yves Saint-Laurent and Jean Paul Gautier. Today, she is an expert in Transformative and Wholistic Learning, an author, and a spiritual guide. Her first and award-winning book, *Living a Spiritual Life in a Material World,* attracted more than one hundred audiences, including a TEDx talk: *You Can Eat Your Cake and Have Enlightenment Too.*

Born in Israel into an alcoholic family, Anna grew up with a severe stutter, undiagnosed learning challenges, and anorexic tendencies. Although she had very low self-esteem, a major shift would transform her circumstances, whisking her away to a ten-year modeling career in Paris. Despite her material success, something was missing. So, Anna returned to school, earning a Ph.D. from the California Institute of Integral Studies, where she concentrated on facilitating transformative learning with individuals and groups. Following a life-changing experience at the Findhorn Foundation in her early forties, she realized her calling to help others experience similar life-changing transformations.

Anna hosts the online Expansive Community, a sacred space for like-minded spirits to practice connecting with our inner divinity, accelerate our spiritual growth, and meet the challenges of our times. In the community, Anna offers self-paced courses, group coaching, and individual mentoring using simple and powerful tools to live a life of purpose and impact, experience deep and nourishing fulfillment, and enjoy the creative beauty and wonder of life.

Anna resides in Sonoma County, California, with her spouse Leon and is fluent in English, Hebrew, French, and Swedish.